W9-BNN-527

HE
CAME
FIRST

OTHER BOOKS BY ROD PARSLEY

HE
FOLLOWING CHRIST TO
CAME
SPIRITUAL BREAKTHROUGH
FIRST

ROD PARSLEY

THOMAS NELSON PUBLISHERS®
Nashville

Published in Nashville, Tennessee, by Thomas Nelson, Inc.

Unless otherwise noted, Scripture quotations are from the KING JAMES VER-
SION.

Scripture quotations noted NASB are from the NEW AMERICAN STANDARD
BIBLE®. © The Lockman Foundation 1960, 1962, 1963, 1968, 1971, 1972, 1973,
1975, 1977. Used by permission.

Scripture quotations noted NIV are from the HOLY BIBLE: NEW INTERNA-
TIONAL VERSION®. Copyright © 1973, 1978, 1984 by International Bible
Society. Used by permission of Zondervan Publishing House. All rights reserved.

Jacket Design: Uttley/DouPonce DesignWorks
www.uddesignworks.com

Cover photo: Stone Images

ISBN 0-7852-6571-6

Printed in the United States of America

01 02 03 04 05 BVG 5 4 3 2 1

CONTENTS

IV. VIGOR:
THE STRENGTH OF THE BREAKER

V. OVERPOWERING WEALTH:
THE CAPACITY OF THE BREAKER

HE
CAME
FIRST

THE FIRST AMONG FIRSTS

For hundreds of years, people said that it couldn't be done; when the Creator of the heavens and the earth fashioned the human body, He did not equip it to break through. People believed it and the record of history confirmed it: Man could not run fast enough to break the 4-minute mile. Until a breaker emerged.

On May 6, 1954, British physician Roger Bannister broke the 4-minute-mile barrier with a time of 3 minutes 59.4 seconds. The world celebrated his record time as a milestone in human achievement and overnight, John Bannister became a household name.

We live in a society enamored with firsts. Television news programs claim, "We bring you the most extensive news coverage *first*." Open the newspaper and daily you will read stories about people attempting to be the first: the first to fly around the world nonstop in a hot-air balloon, the first to swim across the Atlantic Ocean. Some feats are significant and others are trivial, but what matters most is the notoriety of being the first.

Those men and women who successfully break the barriers that confine the rest of the world etch their names in the annals of world history. Those who come in second are usually destined to lives of obscurity. Within two months of Bannister's record-breaking run,

John Landy shaved a second off the world-record time. But few people remember the name John Landy because really, he came second. *John Bannister came first.*

Ask someone to give the name of a person accomplishing a famous first and they may well describe:

- Sir Edmund Hillary and Tenzing Norgay—the first two men to successfully scale Mount Everest, the world's highest mountain

- Robert Peary—the leader of the first team of individuals to reach the North Pole

- Charles Lindbergh and Amelia Earhart—the first man and woman to fly a solo transatlantic flight

- Neil Armstrong – the first man to walk on the moon.

People who win the notoriety of being first lay claim to riches, accolades, and respect. Roger Bannister and Edmund Hillary were both knighted by the royal family in England. Robert Peary was designated Rear Admiral of the United States Navy. Charles Lindbergh was commissioned a colonel in the U.S. Air Service Reserve. And Neil Armstrong was awarded the Presidential Medal of Freedom.

Others, however, continue their quest for further firsts and perish in their attempts. Amelia Earhart presumably died in an airplane crash while attempting to be the first woman to fly an airplane around the world.

Men and women who accomplish these feats of greatness are endowed with the spirit of a breaker. Breakers look at barriers as merely building blocks to further feats of achievement. They refuse to take life at face value, believing that greatness lies beyond the next barrier. With fierce determination and fearless courage, they break through what others believed was impenetrable.

Breakers go before us and prove that it *can* be accomplished. That the barrier *can* be broken. And the rest of the world follows their lead. Within a few short years of Bannister's run, his record was broken sixty-six times by twenty-six different runners.

JESUS WAS THE FIRST OF ALL FIRSTS

But there is one man whose life dwarfs all other feats of greatness. He alone can claim the title as the first of all firsts: Jesus Christ. *He came first.*

Jesus is the Breaker who goes before us. He broke through the barricade separating divinity from humanity, clothing Himself in human flesh. Through His life He showed us how we can reach into the supernatural and bring it back into the natural. Then, after His crucifixion, He broke down the gates of hell, conquering death, disease, and destruction. What Jesus accomplished on our behalf will never be replicated. *He came first.*

God's holy Word describes Jesus as Mary's firstborn son (Luke 2:7). He was born of a virgin, the seed of God planted in Mary's womb. But Jesus' birth was not His beginning. *He came first.* Further in Scripture we read that Jesus is:

- the firstborn over all creation (Col. 1:15).

- the firstborn from the dead (Col. 1:18).

- the firstborn among the brethren (Rom. 8:29).

- the firstfruits of the dead (1 Cor. 15:20).

- the First and the Last (Rev. 22:13).

Before the beginning of creation, Jesus was there, and at the end of the age, Jesus will still be there. Jesus is first, not only in sequence of time, but also in order of importance. Simply put, Jesus is the first of all firsts. *He came first.*

Best of all, if you belong to Jesus, then Jesus, the first of all firsts, lives in you. You are endowed with the seeds of greatness because the seed of the Breaker who goes before us is within you.

In this book you will read about Jesus, the Breaker who goes before us, and you will be equipped with the tools that will take you where even angels fear to tread. Clothed with virtue, valor, vigor, and fearless courage, you will count yourself among the remnant people of God who take back what has been stolen.

Don't settle for second place. Don't be content with a complacent life of mediocre existence that so easily satisfies the people of this present age and more so, the church. You can break the barriers that limit others because we follow in the footsteps of the Breaker who goes before us. You can be a breaker because *He came first.*

PART I

BECOMING
A BREAKER

CHAPTER 1

GOD IS RAISING UP A GENERATION OF BREAKERS

As the hand of God strikes midnight on the timepiece of humanity's climactic consummation, a vestige of valiant men and women is emerging from the masses. This multitude of noble people are resolute in reclaiming their divine authority and walking once again in a new outpouring of Holy Ghost power that will eclipse that of a bygone millennium.

These champions do not stumble at the feet of men stronger than themselves. They neither cower in the face of their critics nor despair over endeavors that fail to meet their expectations. Rather, they engage in the arena of conflict. Their bodies bear the scars of a soldier, their souls attest to an advancing adversary, and their spirits aspire to an unrivaled grandeur, the untold glory, of fighting for a righteous cause.

Greatness is not determined by the amount of money acquired, the level of education attained, or the degree of promotion achieved. The greatness of a person is measured by the cause that propels him forward and the price he is willing to pay—at times sacrificing his very self—to see it fulfilled. Greatness is gauged by devotion to

1

God, dedication to family, and determination on one's knees. To quote Charles de Gaulle, "Nothing great will ever be achieved without great men, and men are great only if they are determined to be so."[1]

These men and women, with character and courage of an uncommon caliber, carry within themselves the spirit of these famous words from Sir Winston Churchill:

> Never give in! Never give in! Never! Never! Never! Never! In anything great or small, large or petty—never give in except to convictions of honor and good sense.[2]

Infused with the anointing, authority, acceptance, and ability of God, these heroic men and women are strategically positioned on the edge of a Holy Ghost revolution. They have come to the kingdom for such a time as this with the purpose of inciting a riot and effecting a divine disturbance in the heart of the church until the reverberation is felt like a shock wave throughout a sin-sick society.

WHAT WE NEED IS A HOLY GHOST INSURRECTION IN THE CHURCH!

The vast majority of our churches are not worthy of these courageous men and women. Far too many pews are filled with shallow, soft Christians who must be spoon-fed a steady diet of spiritual junk food. But how can we blame them when the preacher serving this spiritual pablum was selected with scrutiny by a backslidden church board, not for his prophetic call, but for his Las Vegas ability to lead this personality cult once called the church?

These famished followers of Jesus turn on Christian television looking for spiritual food, and what do they find? Pseudo-Christian charlatans peddling prophecies for a price. Spiritual opportunists of this sort are no different—and no better—than your "psychic friend" on late-night TV.

The order of the day is entertainment, not intercession; comfort, not conviction; and rebellion, not repentance. This social club we call a church is best known for its adultery, not its anointing; its drunkenness, not its sobriety; and its laziness, not its love for lost souls staggering toward the edge of an eternal hell.

Many are more familiar with religious fiction than the foundational pillars of sound doctrine. No wonder our moral and spiritual condition is perilously frail. We've been lulled into a lethargic state of spiritual inertia. We've become weak adherents of a gospel we know nothing of.

Never before has the church stood poised for a move of God. Christians are dying for something more.

GOD IS GOING TO USE YOU FAR BEYOND YOUR WILDEST DREAMS

The time has come for these people of character and courage to rise up. A people who are no longer satisfied with the sickness, poverty, and disease this mortal life brings. A people who are no longer content with church as usual. A people who love no one but God and fear nothing but sin. The time has come for a generation of breakers—a remnant people with undying devotion who follow He who came first, Jesus—to appear who are willing to do whatever it takes to storm the gates of heaven and raze the gates of hell.

Twwenty-five hundred years ago Ezekiel looked through the telescope of prophecy and fixed his eyes on such a generation. He witnessed the day—eventually fulfilled on May 15, 1948—when Israel would be restored as a nation. And just as his prophecy in Ezekiel 36 foretold the restoration of Israel, it also spoke prophetically about the restoration of the church. This age—this last generation—would be a time of favor, blessing, and power for God's people. But the reason for such a great outpouring of His Spirit has nothing to do with you:

> Therefore say unto the house of Israel, Thus saith the LORD GOD;
> I do not this for your sakes, O house of Israel, but for mine holy
> name's sake, which ye have profaned among the heathen, whither
> ye went. (Ezek. 36:22)

God is on the verge of doing something great. He's going to use you in ways far beyond anything you could ever imagine:

- Strolling through the supermarket, a woman passing by is going to be convicted of sin and fall on her knees in front of you pleading, "What must I do to be saved?"

- As you sit in the lobby at the local quick-lube shop waiting for an oil change, God's going to give you a word of knowledge for the person beside you. You're not going to want to share it, but the fire shut up in your bones is going to be so great you won't be able to resist.

- Walking down the sidewalk, people are going to be healed simply because your shadow touched them.

BUT IT'S NOT ABOUT YOU

But understand this: God is not going to do this for your benefit; He's going to do it for His. He's going to use you not because of you but in spite of you. You see, you can't get holy enough for Him to use you because of your good deeds. Even your good works are like filthy rags (see Isa. 64:6). What God is about to perform has nothing to do with you and everything to do with Him.

God then explains His motivation:

And I will sanctify my great name, which was profaned among the heathen, which ye have profaned in the midst of them; *and the heathen shall know that I am the* LORD, saith the Lord GOD. (Ezek. 36:23, italics added)

The children of Israel had profaned God's name. To profane literally means "to pierce or wound, often using a sword."[3] The lifestyles of the people who claimed to know God showed no visible demonstration of the invisible God. The surrounding nations were no different than God's chosen people. In fact, they were driving people *away* from Him. For this reason God said He would sanctify Himself inside his lifeless church *so that He might display His mighty name among the heathen.*

This powerless church, which has given the world every reason to reject an all-powerful God, will rise up. You see, through our trials God has gained the attention of the world. People today look at the church and say, "You've served God for nothing. What difference does living for Jesus make?"

Satan asked the same question when he presented himself before the throne of God: "Have you looked at Job?"

"Yes, I have."

"He serves you for naught. And if you lift your hand off him, he'll curse you."

But in his darkest hour, when he had nowhere else to turn, Job responded: "Though he slay me, yet will I trust in him" (Job 13:15). And God redeemed Job's life. In the same way, when the church seems to be at its worst, we can trust that God will deliver us. But He's not going to do it for our sakes, He's going to do it to show His name great to *all* the people of the earth.

When is God going to do this? When He gathers Israel back to its homeland:

> For I will take you from among the heathen, and gather you out of all countries, and will bring you into your own land. (Ezek. 36:24)

Friends, we are living in the same generation that Israel was restored! This is the generation when God's Word is going to be fulfilled! God is going to use us, but it won't be because of us. Now watch what comes next:

> Then will I sprinkle clean water upon you, and ye shall be clean: from all your filthiness, and from all your idols, will I cleanse you. A new heart also will I give you, and a new spirit will I put within you: and I will take away the stony heart out of your flesh, and I will give you an heart of flesh. And I will put my spirit within you, *and cause you to walk in my statutes*, and ye shall keep my judgments, and do them. (Ezek. 36:25–27, italics added)

God said He would cleanse us and replace our hearts of stone with hearts of flesh. Then He promised He would put His Spirit—His breath, His life—within us. And what would this Spirit do to us? It would cause us to walk in His statutes. The best translation of the word *cause* is "to make."[4] The Holy Spirit is going to make us follow Him.

GOD IS RAISING UP A PEOPLE POSSESSED BY THE HOLY GHOST

God is giving birth to a revolutionary people who are going to be possessed by an irresistible power. The book of Acts is going to be reenacted before our very eyes. In fact, we're not going to be able to help ourselves because, as we yield ourselves to the power of the Holy Ghost, He is going to do it through us. We'll just be along for the ride!

To this generation God will give the power to

- overcome sin and bad habits.

- cast out devils.

- call for angelic protection.

- heal the sick.

- destroy the works of Satan.

- experience an answer to every prayer.

- work miracles.

- execute judgment.

- expose false prophets.

- receive abundant provision for life.

- take authority over the devil.

- move in revelation knowledge.

- possess healing and divine health.

- receive the gifts of the Holy Ghost and impart those gifts to others.

- walk in the fruit of the Spirit.

Does this sound too good to be true? To the ordinary Christian it is. But to the breakthrough generation, God's remnant people, it isn't. Now please don't misunderstand, the ordinary Christian who confesses Jesus Christ as Lord and Savior is still going to heaven. But throughout Scripture, God has shown a precedent of working through a remnant people: a Samuel, a David, an Elijah, a Daniel. These are people whose faces are set like flint to please God in the face of public opinion. These are people who possess the spirit of the breaker.

GOD IS GATHERING A REMNANT OF BREAKERS

One hundred and fifty years before Ezekiel's prophecy, the prophet Micah described the same event:

> I will surely assemble, O Jacob, all of thee; I will surely gather the remnant of Israel; I will put them together as the sheep of Bozrah, as the flock in the midst of their fold: they shall make great noise by reason of the multitude of men. (Mic. 2:12)

At the same time that Jacob—another name for Israel—is assembled, a remnant will also be gathered. Amid the great outpouring of God's Spirit in this last generation, a remnant people is also being gathered. And you can see it in the church: Some people are passionate for God, while others love God, but they wouldn't necessarily describe themselves as passionate. God didn't say they weren't Israel; He just said they weren't the remnant.

The word God uses to describe this remnant is *flock*. A flock is a group of sheep. In fact, this passage describes it as a "flock in the midst of their fold." It was a flock within a flock.

And out of this flock came a great noise. The vast multitude was so great that their bleating sounded like a roar. And what was it that caused such a commotion?

> The breaker is come up before them: they have broken up, and have passed through the gate, and are gone out by it: and their king shall pass before them, and the LORD on the head of them. (Mic. 2:13)

Jesus, the Prince of breakers, is leading His flock of breakers through the gates that have bound them for centuries!

THE SONS OF PEREZ WERE ANOINTED BREAKERS

One hundred and fifty years after Ezekiel, God called Nehemiah, an Israelite in captivity in Persia, to return to Jerusalem to repair the protective wall surrounding the city. Without it, the city was vulnerable to attack from even the weakest enemy. After resisting a great deal of opposition from Sanballat and his henchmen, Nehemiah and the Jewish men of the city were successful.

After their celebration, the leaders drew lots to determine which people from the surrounding rural areas would inhabit the Holy City. Here is a partial but telling list of spiritual leaders—priests, Levites, and temple servants from the tribe of Judah—who were selected:

> And at Jerusalem dwelt certain of the children of Judah, and of the children of Benjamin. Of the children of Judah; Athaiah the son of Uzziah, the son of Zechariah, the son of Amariah, the son of Shephatiah, the son of Mahalaleel, of the children of Perez; and Maaseiah the son of Baruch, the son of Colhozeh, the son of Hazaiah, the son of Adaiah, the son of Joiarib, the son of Zechariah, the son of Shiloni. All the sons of Perez that dwelt at Jerusalem *were* four hundred threescore and eight valiant men. (Neh. 11:4–6)

This may seem like a meaningless list of names—until you understand the meaning of two names in particular: Mahalaleel and Perez. There are two Mahalaleels and two Perezes in Scripture. Because they were both from the tribe of Judah, we know they were related in some way. But the other Mahalaleel and Perez mentioned in Scripture were even more closely related. More on that a little later.

Mahalaleel means "praise of God." But this isn't just praise of any god, it's the praise of *Elohim*, the Hebrew term used when referring to almighty God. The name Elohim paints the picture of a ram who relentlessly butts his head until he breaks through. Our praise releases the power of God to break through anything that stands in our way!

A second name in this passage is of even greater significance: Perez. This passage tells us that Perez had 468 sons. Of course, Perez wasn't the natural father of these 468 men; they were descendants of one great man. And the defining characteristic of these men, what distinguished them from other men, was that they were valiant. They were men fit for service and able to defend the breach. *The sons of Perez were men of valor, of fearless courage.*

The name Perez means "to break through," "to break down," or "to burst." It is the same word used in reference to Jesus in Micah 2:13, which we looked at a moment ago. Variations of this word indicate that the significance does not mean simply to punch a hole through a barrier but to level it or raze it. *The sons of Perez were men of great vigor, or strength.*

This word is also used in reference to increase—an indication of the material blessing from God. In other words, these men of valor, these men of vigor, were also men of great means. *The sons of Perez were men of great wealth* by reason of their ability to use the resources God placed in their hands.

Because the sons of Perez were spiritual leaders among the Jews, we know that they lived lives that were sanctified, set apart for God. *The sons of Perez were men of virtue.*

One interesting note: The Hebrew term for *breach* also comes from this same word. The sons of Perez were repairers of the breach as well as creators of new breaches. They repaired the walls of the Holy City, but they also broke through any walls that stood in their way.

The sons of Perez refused to cave in to popular opinion. They were men anointed by God to break through any barriers that stood in the way of God's promise to Israel. They were men who refused to take no for an answer if they knew there was a yes from God. They were relentless.

WE ARE SONS AND DAUGHTERS OF PEREZ

Which would you rather have in Jerusalem—Perez, or the 468 sons of Perez? His sons, of course! It's better to have 468 Perezes repairing the breach and breaking through barriers than just one. But God isn't finished anointing more sons, and daughters, of Perez.

God had a son—his name was Adam. Adam had two sons, Cain and Abel. Cain slew Abel and Eve said, "Give me a son to replace Abel," so God gave her another son, through Adam, named Seth. Seth had a son named Mahalaleel. Remember that name? It means "praise of the God that breaks through."

Mahalaleel had a son whose name was Enoch. We know that Enoch walked with God, and he was not, for God took him. Enoch had a son whose name was Methuselah. Methuselah had a son; his name was Noah. Noah had a son who had a son, and so on, and his name was Abraham. Abraham had a son; his name was Isaac. Isaac had a son; his name was Jacob. Jacob had twelve sons, one of whom was named Judah, which means "praise." Judah had a son, *whose name was Perez.*

Perez had a son who had a son, and so on, whose name was Joseph. Joseph had a son whose name was Jesus. If you belong to Jesus Christ, you have been adopted into the family of God. You are one of Jesus' brothers or sisters, and you now have His spiritual genealogy. You are endowed with the spirit of the breaker, because Romans 8:29 says, "For whom he did foreknow, he also did predestinate to be conformed to the image of his Son, that he might be the firstborn among many brethren."

Everything that God accomplished in the First Adam and everything that Satan altered in him afterward, God corrected in the Second Adam—Jesus. And through the intervening power of the Holy Ghost, God has endowed you with the spirit of the breaker to return this fallen world to the original state of affairs and to take dominion over this earth.

YOU'RE A THIRD-DAY CHRISTIAN

We have entered a new millennium that bears great significance to the church. Although this century is numbered by the 2000s, it is actually the third millennium. We now live in the third day. Three is the number of the Holy Ghost, the third person of the Trinity. We live in an age that will experience the power of the Holy Ghost as none have before.

Three is also the number of resurrection: Jesus was resurrected on the third day. We live in an age when the church, the body of Christ, will be resurrected and restored as never before.

You're a third-day Christian. You have available to you the resurrection power of Jesus Christ to break through the insidious evil of this sinful world and the lethargy of a sleeping church. God has anointed you to take up the mantle of the breaker, if you choose to accept it—to take dominion over this world and bring restoration to the church.

THE MANTLE OF THE BREAKER
IS NOW IN YOUR HANDS

Through this book I place into your hands the mantle of the breaker. And through such great men as Howard Carter, Smith

Wigglesworth, and Lester Sumrall, God has anointed me to impart this spiritual truth to you. As you read, you will discover the characteristics of the breaker:

- Virtue

- Valor

- Vigor

- Overpowering wealth

If you can catch the heart of what God is saying, by the time you're finished reading this book, you're going to have the tenacity to break down any door that Satan may have closed in front of you. Complacency, bondage, addiction, sickness, depression, and poverty will be broken in your life. You're going to spread your wings like an eagle and fly!

The rest of our time together, I will impart to you what God has made real in my life. But first, we're going to look at Jesus, the Prince of breakers, the Lion of the tribe of Judah, and then we are going to learn how to access the power of the breaker.

CHAPTER 2

THE BREAKER WHO
GOES BEFORE US

In the beginning, God existed in a vacuum of self-awareness and self-existence. He searched among the citizens of eternity for a comrade, a confidant, a companion—a friend. And He found none among the citizens of eternity, so our Canaan King created man out of the cold, red clay of earth, and there He built for His creation a home. And He dwelt with him there in the elegant Garden of Eden.

Man and God were one. Adam and Eve fellowshipped freely with their Father in the brilliance of paradise. Their relationship was one of reckless abandon. No reassurances were needed, and with the cool breeze of eternity blowing across their brows, Adam and Eve heard those words: "Who shall separate us from the love of God?"

What a God and what a garden! Everything pleasing to the eye and pleasant to the taste. The happy splashing fountain of life. Bougainvillea and amaranth blooming everywhere. Animals walking in kindness with one another.

But you know the story. Right there in the middle of paradise, Adam, God's created son, and Eve sided with God's great archenemy, Lucifer. The boldest rebellion ever known had just begun.

God came down to earth and with flaming sword banished the man and his wife to the eastern plains of sterile Eden. The image of God had been dashed to pieces. Adam and Eve were now marked with these grisly words: *death* and *the grave*.

SIN ERECTED AN IMPENETRABLE BARRIER

Man divorced himself from the divine when he refused to flee from the entanglements of evil. Lust conceived—the allure of being like God—had produced sin. Satan's enticing promise of knowing good from evil had been fulfilled. But it didn't enable Adam and Eve to be like God. Instead, the knowledge of every evil atrocity and abomination filled their beings. And, they were endowed with an acute awareness of everything good that lay just beyond their sin-infected reach.

Yet in the hollowness of their hearts, these words resounded: "Blessed are the pure in heart, for they shall see God." The pure had become polluted. The man and his wife successfully separated themselves from God, forming an impenetrable barrier between the Creator and His creation. Only the Prince of breakers would be able to breach this barricade of sin.

Scripture tells us, "There is a way which seemeth right unto a man, but the end thereof are the ways of death" (Prov. 14:12). Man did what *he* thought was right, but in the end it resulted in death and separation from God.

Exposure to Satan's corruption carried with it the communicable disease called sin, contaminating the bloodstream of all humanity. As a result, lawlessness lorded over the land. Satan successfully separated humanity from their very substance and sustenance of life—God the Creator. Man missed the mark, sin became the standard, and death became the decree. And out of the emptiness, hurt, and brokenheartedness, God cried out, "It was My friend who forsook Me."

WHAT IS SIN?

Not long ago, I was awakened from my sleep by a disturbing dream. Men and women were being dragged by their feet, screaming, into the smoke-filled corridors of the doomed and the damned. They weren't entering hell for a moment or two, for a weekend retreat, but for the endless eons of eternity. For ages upon endless ages they would experience the torment of pain and regret from the cackling bowels of the devil's hell. Men and women were desperately grasping for the edge of the crevasse as they plunged headlong into an eternal hell that was created not for them, but for the devil and his angels.

"God, what caused this?" I asked.

"Sin. All the work of sin," He replied. The weeping that had jarred me from my sleep now turned to gut-wrenching sobs.

"But God," I cried out, "what is sin?"

"Take a pen and begin to write," He answered. And this is what I wrote:

Sin is the cut of a knife. The fear in a scream. The hollowness of an empty stomach. The pretentiousness of pride, the clutch of cancer, the malice of murder. It's the clamor of war, the helplessness of divorce. Sin is an epidemic called AIDS. It's the blank stare in the face of the homeless.

Sin is the dollar bill in the pocket of the abortion doctor. The despair of poverty. The fear of the past, present, and future. It's the sob of a little girl, alone in her bedroom nursing a bruised cheek, tears staining her lace-trimmed pillow because her drunken daddy slapped her just hours before.

Sin is the federal penitentiary, and arguing, lying, and cheating. It's the deceitfulness of earthly security. It's stealing and insanity, heresy, prejudice, and suicide. Sin is the occult, New Age deceit, pagan religion, and religious tradition. It's demon possession and sirens and hospitals. It's the silence of death, the cold reality of a funeral, and the necessity of an eternal hell.

Sin is the whispering of friends. It's the drive that fuels sexual perversion, homosexuality, rape, and incest. It's the bondage of alcohol and drug addiction. It's everything cruel and painful. It's every curse, blight, and plague known in human history.

And to satisfy sin's ceaseless appetite, men and women sell their souls. Many will spend an eternity in hell trying to pay the price for something they will never be able to afford.

CAN GOD *REALLY* REDEEM OUR LIVES?

Reflecting on the heinousness of sin, the apostle Paul asked the question that has plagued humanity since the beginning of time: "Who shall deliver me from the body of this death?" (Rom. 7:24).

The answer? Jesus Christ, the Breaker who goes before us. He is the Lion of the tribe of Judah. The root of Jesse. The branch of David. The resurrected Canaan King who passed through the very bowels of hell and emerged on the victory side of an empty tomb. He's the son of Perez who broke through the penalty of death and the power of sin. He's the repairer of the breach who rebuilt, restored, and revived the broken relationship between a timeless God and a temporal man.

Yet despite God's great condescension to earth, in the recesses of our hearts we so often ask ourselves, *Can God redeem my life?*

Let's return to Micah 2:12–13 for a moment:

> I will surely assemble, O Jacob, all of thee; I will surely gather the remnant of Israel; I will put them together as the sheep of Bozrah, as the flock in the midst of their fold: they shall make great noise by reason of the multitude of men. The breaker is come up before them: they have broken up, and have passed through the gate, and

are gone out by it: and their king shall pass before them, and the LORD on the head of them.

Notice how God begins: "*Surely*, O Jacob, I will assemble all of thee. *Surely*, I will gather the remnant of Israel." Whenever a divine edict is declared in Scripture, God uses a double annunciation. A double annunciation is the repetition of a word or phrase in order to emphasize its forcefulness. So when God says, "Surely, surely," He double-time means surely. He leaves no room for "maybe so," "might be so," or a "someday so." In other words, He was saying, "You can count on it."

GOD WON'T LEAVE YOU OUT

Now, let's look at what God said: "Surely, O Jacob, *I will assemble all of thee.*" Let me give you my translation of this phrase: "God isn't going to leave anyone out." When He gathers His church, there isn't any sin condition or skin condition that is beyond His reach. It doesn't matter if

- your skin color is black, brown, red, beige, or lily white.
- you're short, tall, or in between.
- you stuck a heroin needle in your arm last night.
- you walked the streets yesterday and sold your body for a $20 bill.
- you've played church all your life but you still don't know if you're going to heaven.
- you have a secret life that only you and God know about.

God won't leave you out.
People say, "I'm not good enough to be accepted by God." But

God answers, "[I'm] not willing that any should perish, but that all should come to repentance" (2 Peter 3:9). *God won't leave you out.*

Others say, "I can't be good enough to be a Christian." But God answers, "But God commendeth his love toward us, in that, *while we were yet sinners*, Christ died for us" (Rom. 5:8, italics added). *God won't leave you out.*

Still others say, "I'll never be good enough to be used by God." But God answers, "My grace is sufficient for thee: for my strength is made perfect in weakness" (2 Cor. 12:9). *God won't leave you out.*

It doesn't matter what you've done, what's been done to you, or what you're facing tomorrow—God is not about to leave you out.

THE BREAKER IS OUR LIBERATOR AND LEADER

In this passage in Micah, we see a prophetic picture of Jesus as the Liberator and Leader. He liberates the sheep, breaking through the bonds that hold them captive. What was once the warrant of death has now become the passport to life. He gathers the remnant and leads them out of their bondage and into freedom.

Have you ever seen a dog that has spent all of his life anchored to a chain? At first the dog tries to break loose from the bondage, but discovering that the chain is stronger than he is, he gives up. He knows where his boundaries are and he sees no need to test them. You could remove the chain from the dog's collar, but the dog sees no need to break free. He remains captive to what no longer exists. The dog has been liberated but not led.

Such is the existence of the vast majority of Christians in this world. We have all been anchored to sin, and Jesus has broken our chains. He's our Liberator. But to many, He's not their Leader. Refusing to follow Him beyond the safe confines of a familiar but pitiful past, they grow content with a life of bondage, poverty, and sickness.

"I am come that they might have life," Jesus said in John 10:10, "and that they might have it more abundantly." The Breaker who goes before us came to liberate us and lead us out of our bondage.

What drives Him to be the Breaker on our behalf? He's the sinner's best friend. Jesus declared, "I am the way, the truth, and the life: no man cometh unto the Father, but by me" (John 14:6). Jesus is our bondage breaker and way maker. He's the "friend that sticketh closer than a brother" (Prov. 18:24). He's not just any Breaker; He's *your* Breaker.

JESUS PROVED HE IS YOUR BREAKER THROUGH HIS INCARNATION

God could have watched us from afar, striking us with bolts of lightning at the hint of any misstep or misdeed. But He didn't. He could have kept His hands clean from the stain of our humanity. But He didn't.

Laying down His omnipotence, omniscience, and omnipresence, Jesus removed His royal crown, laid down His scepter, and announced, "If I'm going to set you free, I need to be one in humanity with you." And Jesus broke through the safe haven of heaven and entered our fallen world.

In order to penetrate the seemingly impenetrable wall of separation, God knew He needed to purchase man with the blood of His only Son. It had to be spotless blood. Sinless blood. And so Jesus leaped into the womb of a young virgin girl and was born in an earthly manger while the angels sang happy birthday and the shepherds stood by as witnesses to the momentous event.

Jesus wasn't born into a family of privilege. He didn't trumpet His divinity to His Jewish countrymen. God's Word tells us that He "made himself of no reputation, and took upon him the form of a servant" (Phil. 2:7). His birthplace was a little cow town whose only claim to fame was that it had been the hometown of Israel's greatest king *one thousand years earlier.*

Rather, Jesus was born to parents of meager means. The apostle Paul writes that Jesus "made himself of no reputation, and took upon him the form of a servant, and was made in the likeness of men: and being found in fashion as a man, he humbled himself, and became obedient unto death, even the death of the cross" (Phil 2:7–8).

Although He was God, Jesus grew up very human. He experienced sorrow, frustration, temptation, hunger, thirst, and anger.

God stuck His arm elbow-deep into the muck and mire of our mess and brought us out by the death of His own Son. We have no right to say, "God doesn't understand my problems" because Jesus broke through the barrier separating humanity from divinity:

> For we have not an high priest which cannot be touched with the feeling of our infirmities; but was in all points tempted like as we are, yet without sin. (Heb. 4:15)

Despite His humble beginnings, Jesus manifested a mastery over demons, depravity, disease, and eventually death itself.

JESUS PROVED HE IS YOUR BREAKER
THROUGH HIS ASSOCIATION WITH SINNERS

Clothing Himself in humanity should have been enough humiliation for Jesus, but it wasn't. Having given up so much in order to come to earth, He could have whiled away His time discussing the finer points of theology with the religious elite, but He didn't. What irritated the spiritual leaders of Jesus' time was that He kept breaking through the barrier dividing the spiritual haves from the spiritual have-nots. And what irritated Jesus was that so many people worked so hard to keep that barrier in place:

> But whereunto shall I liken this generation? It is like unto children sitting in the markets, and calling unto their fellows, and

saying, We have piped unto you, and ye have not danced; we have mourned unto you, and ye have not lamented. For John came neither eating nor drinking, and they say, He hath a devil. The Son of man came eating and drinking, and they say, Behold a man gluttonous, and a winebibber, a friend of publicans and sinners. (Matt. 11:16–19)

Like a magnet to metal, Jesus was drawn to the heart of the sinner. While the rest of Israel avoided the spiritual half-breed Samaritans at any cost, Jesus chose to walk through Samaria in the middle of the day and minister to an outcast of the outcasts.

Sitting down at a well, He met a woman who had been married five times and was living with a man who wasn't even her husband. The other Samaritan women wouldn't let her draw water with them in the cool of the morning, so she was forced to go to the well in the heat of the day.

"Would you give Me a drink?" Jesus asked the woman as He wiped the sweat from His brow.

Astonished, she replied, "Why would you, a Jewish man, want me, a Samaritan woman, to give you a drink?"

"If you knew who I was, you would ask Me for a drink of living water," Jesus answered. By the time Jesus finished His drink, the woman had already run to a nearby town and brought her outcast friends to meet Jesus.

At a time when the Jewish religious leaders believed God could care less about the Samaritans, Jesus held revival meetings among these untouchables for three days (see John 4:1–42)!

Jesus Proved He Is Your Breaker Through His Preaching

Jesus not only proved He was your Breaker through His incarnation and His association with sinners, but He also proved it through

His preaching. He articulated the love and holiness of God with power like no one in human history. His preaching broke through the caricature of dead religion, planting the seeds of the gospel into the hearts of His listeners. Then, on Pentecost Sunday, those seeds were watered by the Holy Spirit, yielding fruit that continues to this day.

To the sinner He preached the love of God. In a three-part sermon in Luke 15, He explained the heart of a God who desires to restore the friendship that was broken as a result of Adam's and Eve's sin.

In His first parable, Jesus painted a picture of a shepherd who left his flock of ninety-nine and searched throughout the country-side to find a single lost sheep that had wandered off. In the second part of His sermon, Jesus shared about a woman who lost a coin and searched every crack and crevice until she found it. Finally, He told the story of the prodigal son who broke his father's heart, left home, and spent his inheritance on wine, women, and song. Yet, when the son finally came to his senses and decided to return home, his father accepted him with open arms and received him back as a son.

In each parable Jesus illustrated that all of us have wandered away from God. Yet God searches for us and when He finds us, He not only restores us, but He throws a party to celebrate our return.

To the religious He preached the holiness of God. No one was harder on the religious leaders than Jesus. He called the Pharisees blind guides, hypocrites, snakes, and "whited sepulchres" (see Matt. 23:13–39). The holiness Jesus preached consisted of more than just the nobility of one's actions. It was based upon the purity of one's heart. Jesus equated lust with adultery and hate with murder.

JESUS PROVED HE IS YOUR BREAKER
THROUGH HIS PRAYERS

Jesus' ministry was singularly focused on one objective: bringing salvation to the world. He didn't lament the riches and comforts of heaven that He forfeited in order to come to earth. He didn't use

His divine powers to impress His fellow Jews. Rather, Jesus sought to break through the wall that existed between God and humanity:

> But your iniquities have separated between you and your God, and your sins have hid his face from you, that he will not hear. (Isa. 59:2)

Because the pretentiousness of our sins drowned out our prayers in the ears of a holy God, Jesus interceded on our behalf. He took up our cause as His own and represented us before the Father.

On the night He was betrayed, sweat dripped from Jesus' brow like blood as He prayed that God would preserve His fragile flock of followers. But He also prayed for those people who would someday be brought into the kingdom as a result of these people:

> Neither pray I for these alone, but for them also which shall believe on me through their word. (John 17:20)

The night He was nailed to the cross, Jesus not only prayed for His disciples, He prayed for you! Jesus didn't prove He was just a Breaker, He proved that He was *your* Breaker.

Then, hanging on the cross between two criminals, with an angry mob jeering at Him and the Roman soldiers casting lots for His clothing, He cried out to His Father and prayed, "Father, forgive them; for they know not what they do" (Luke 23:34). At that moment Jesus had every right to think only of Himself:

- He had been nailed to a cross on false charges in the greatest miscarriage of justice in world history.

- His Father had turned His face away from Jesus for the first time in eternity for taking the sins of the world on His shoulders.

- His crucifixion yielded the most excruciating pain of any death known to man.

- His nakedness was exposed for everyone around to see, adding shame to His sorrow and pain.

Jesus had been beaten, betrayed, abased, and abandoned. But the Breaker who goes before us set aside His own well-being in order to remember the sin-stained names of humanity before the Father.

JESUS PROVED HE IS YOUR BREAKER
THROUGH HIS DEATH AND CRUCIFIXION

You're just outside the city of Jerusalem, and your eyes strain to see what lies ahead in the morning fog. The hazy image looks more like an animal than a man. His hair is matted and soaked in blood; His eyes are swollen. Slowly He lifts His head as He strains to see through the blood and sweat on His way to the flogging post. He staggers, His hands bound behind him. You hear the hiss and the whir of the cat-o'-nine-tails as it whistles through the air, and with its claws, reaches and tears the flesh from His back. The Breaker was doing it for you.

His flesh hangs like ribbons around His legs. Three times He falls under the weight of the cross as He walks the lonely *Via Dolorosa*—Latin for "the way of sorrows"—up to Golgotha. The ringing of the hammer is heard as nails part sinew and flesh. His muscles jerk in spasms of horror. You turn your face away but turn back as you hear Him speaking to the thief hanging on the cross beside Him, "Today you'll be with Me in paradise." Tears well up in your eyes as you witness the power of love in action.

"*Eli, Eli, lama sabachthani?* My God, My God, why hast Thou forsaken Me?" Jesus cries out. The God who carpets the valley in green and feeds the baby ravens turned His back on His Son and made darkness Jesus' pavilion. Then it's all over. Jesus is dead.

The cross was lowered to the ground with a sickening thud, jarring the lifeless body of the Prince of God. Lightning flashed overhead and, although it was noon, the sky was pitch-black, for the sun had gone into mourning.

Jesus' corpse was removed from the cross and then clad in grave clothes. Weeping, His followers then placed Him in a tomb.

On that dark day we call Good Friday, hell did its worst to heaven's best. Jesus suffered for you in order to break the grip of sickness and sin on your life.

JESUS PROVED HE IS YOUR BREAKER THROUGH HIS RESURRECTION

If we conclude this story with Jesus' death on the cross, we would have to call Him a liar. He tried. He was a good man, but He failed to break through the curse that Adam and Eve thrust upon humanity. But fortunately, the story continues:

> As it began to dawn toward the first day of the week, came Mary Magdalene and the other Mary to see the sepulchre. And, behold, there was a great earthquake: for the angel of the Lord descended from heaven, and came and rolled back the stone from the door, and sat upon it. His countenance was like lightning and his raiment white as snow: And for fear of him the keepers did shake, and became as dead men. And the angel answered and said unto the women, Fear not ye: for I know that ye seek Jesus, which was crucified. He is not here: for he is risen, as he said. (Matt. 28:1–6)

The Breaker has come and defeated sin, sickness, poverty, death, and the grave! Jesus proved once and for all that no principality or power has mastery over His preeminence.

JESUS PROVED HE IS YOUR BREAKER THROUGH HIS ASCENSION

Jesus not only proved He was your Breaker by virtue of His resurrection, but also by virtue of His ascension. After His resurrection, Jesus entered again the pavilions of heaven. He took His seat at the right hand of the Father, placed the golden crown back on His head, and then picked up His royal scepter to rule once more.

But do you know what He's doing? He's taking your polluted name upon His lips, calling out your name to God and saying, "Father, I know they're guilty, but My blood has paid their price in full."

> Who is he that condemneth? It is Christ that died, yea rather, that is risen again, who is even at the right hand of God, who also maketh intercession for us. (Rom. 8:34)

The Breaker is *still* going before you!

TRUSTING YOUR LIFE TO THE BREAKER

From the cradle to the grave, Jesus is the Breaker who goes before us. There is no experience, no difficulty, no temptation, and no lack that He doesn't understand and that He hasn't provided a way through. Jesus is your Liberator and Leader.

When life is over and you stand at the threshold of death, He promises that He won't leave you. When you cross from this world to the other, you will walk a well-trodden path, for the Breaker has gone before you. So there's nothing to fear.

If you haven't given your life yet to Jesus, now is as good a time as any to do it. Say yes to God and no to the devil. Yes to blessing, no to cursing. Yes to heaven, and no to hell.

What do you have to give up to be a Christian? Poverty, sickness, and sin. When Jesus rose from the grave on Easter morning, He broke the very chains of death in order to set you free. All He's waiting for is you to say yes.

If Jesus is knocking at the door of your heart and you want to give Him control of your life, then pray this prayer:

> *Dear Jesus, I come to You and admit that I am a sinner. Thank You for being the sinner's friend and for dying for me so that I could be free. I repent of my sins and give the control of my life to You. Today I accept You as my Savior and Lord. Fill me with Your Holy Spirit. Show me Your ways, and I will live for You as You show me how. Give me the assurance now that I'm on my way to heaven, and I'll thank You for it the rest of my life. Amen.*

If you just prayed this prayer, here are three things I want you to begin doing right now:

1. *Pray.* It doesn't have to be pretty. If all you say is "help," that will be sufficient for now. Just talk to Him as you would your best friend, except He's better than your best friend.

2. *Get connected in a church that preaches the Word of God.* When you find one, be there every time the doors are open. You need to hear the Word of God preached, and you need the fellowship of the people of God.

3. *Get a Bible and read it.* Begin in the book of 1 John. (You'll learn more about the power of God's Word in the next chapter.)

CHAPTER 3

ACCESSING THE BREAKER'S POWER

Long ago in Asia Minor, King Gordius of Phrygia tethered a wagon to a pole with an extremely intricate knot. Then the king's oracle announced that only a great man, a man capable of ruling all of Asia, would be able to untie it. People throughout Asia Minor traveled to the city where the wagon stood and attempted to unravel the convoluted rope. However, all their efforts were fruitless.

During Alexander the Great's conquest to rule the civilized world, he and his troops arrived in the city where the wagon—and the intricate knot—stood. The people, hoping their city would be spared from his troops, told him the story of the knot. Would he be able to untie it? Would the people be spared?

Alexander the Great examined the knot ever so closely. He looked at it from above, then from below; he followed the rope with his hands from one end to the other and then he stepped back to evaluate the problem. The townspeople waited in anticipation to see how he would respond. Slowly Alexander the Great reached into his sheath, pulled out his sword, and with one great blow, he severed the knot. And Alexander continued his conquest of Asia, which he eventually, and inevitably, accomplished. Since that day, 350 years before Christ, the Gordian knot has become symbolic of an extremely complicated problem that is nearly impossible to solve.

Like the townspeople in the story, we face problems that seem beyond our ability to overcome. But when we are infused with the spirit of the breaker, we can reach into our sheath, pull out the sword of the Spirit, which is the Word of God, and with one mighty swing, we can sever any tie that binds us.

Up to this point, we have studied what a breaker is and how Jesus made a way for you and me to be breakers. But knowing what a breaker is and actually becoming one are entirely different things. The rest of the book will explain how you can be a son or daughter of Perez. In this chapter I will place in your hands the sword that will enable you to break through any tie that binds you. The four sections that follow—virtue, valor, vigor, and overpowering wealth—will be the fruit of the principles of this foundational chapter at work in your life.

BREAKERS ARE NORMAL PEOPLE LIVING IN AN ABNORMAL WORLD

When you look around at the world we live in, do you ever feel out of place? Crime, violence, sexual immorality, sickness and disease, tragedy. There's little evidence of control or restraint, and no sense of the brooding presence of the Holy Spirit guiding us into the good and convicting us of evil. We are living in a society where right has been wrong for so long that righteousness is now considered abnormal.

But know this: We are not abnormal people living in a normal world. We are normal people living in an abnormal world. Even after the fall of Adam and Eve in the Garden, when sin drove its stake into the soul of all mankind, this is still our Father's world. "The earth is the LORD's, and the fulness thereof; the world, and they that dwell therein" (Ps. 24:1). This is not Satan's world, or Washington, D.C.'s world, or Hollywood, California's world. This is not your world or my world. This is our Father's world.

The *normal* Christian life is devoid of crime, violence, sexual immorality, sickness, disease, and tragedy. Addictions to pornography, alcohol, or drugs are, in reality, like that knot, which can be permanently severed with the sword of the Spirit. Yet we continue to examine it, trying to figure out how it can be unraveled. We weren't anointed to analyze it; we were anointed to annihilate it! We're possessed by the Holy Ghost!

LIKE FATHER, LIKE SON OR DAUGHTER

If this is truly our Father's world, have you ever wondered why God still allows evil to flourish? If God is in control, then why do the righteous so often fall short of victory and success? Let me help you: It has nothing to do with God and everything to do with us.

> God said, Let us make man in our image, after our likeness: and let them have dominion over the fish of the sea, and over the fowl of the air, and over the cattle, and over all the earth, and over every creeping thing that creepeth upon the earth. So God created man in his own image, in the image of God created he him; male and female created he them. (Gen. 1:26–27)

Notice that when God created man, He referred to Himself as *us*. Who is "us"? The three persons of the Trinity: Father, Son, and Holy Ghost. We were created as an extension of God. Not that we are literally God, but we *are* Godlike. In fact, this passage says that Adam and Eve were created in the image of God.

What does *image* mean? The Hebrew word means "likeness" or "resemblance."[1] Just as God consists of three persons, so we resemble Him in that we also consist of three parts: body, soul, and spirit.

THE SOURCE OF GOD'S POWER: AGREEMENT

Why is God so ultimately powerful? Because He is in absolute agreement within Himself. During His earthly ministry, Jesus made it clear that He was going about His Father's business (Luke 2:49). He only spoke what the Father told Him to speak (John 12:49), and He only ministered where the Father was already at work (John 5:19). When He healed, He didn't do so by His own power, but by the power of the Holy Spirit (Acts 10:38). At the same time, the Holy Spirit only speaks what He is told to speak (John 16:13). In fact, Jesus concluded His time in the Garden of Gethsemane, just moments before being arrested, by praying this prayer:

> And the glory which thou gavest me I have given them; that they may be one, even as we are one: I in them, and thou in me, that they may be made perfect in one; and that the world may know that thou hast sent me, and hast loved them, as thou hast loved me. (John 17:22–23)

Jesus prayed that the church would be one just as He and the Father are One. When we, the body of Christ, are one, then the world will know Jesus is the Son of God. What fuels the power of God? He is in agreement with Himself! What fuels the power of God in *our* lives? Agreement.

But we can't seem to get into agreement with other believers. Look around you. Churches everywhere are bickering. People who call themselves Christians fight about what color to paint the windowsills outside the church. Other churches split because one half of the congregation wants to sing hymns and the other half wants to sing choruses. Christians in our churches are dying right now because brothers and sisters in Christ are fighting one another when they should be fighting their common enemy: Satan. It's no wonder the church is so powerless!

We can't get into agreement with ourselves. Our churches are filled with people who love God but are led by their feelings. They know they're supposed to love their neighbor, but they struggle with their temper and say things they shouldn't. They know they're supposed to tithe, but they spend what rightfully belongs to God on pleasures and useless stuff that's all going to burn at the end of the age. They know they should be in church, but they reason to themselves, *I've worked so hard and I'm so tired, I think I'll just skip church this week and relax.*

We can't get into agreement with God. How can we come into agreement with God when we don't know His Word and haven't allowed His Word to work in our lives?

WE ARE CREATED IN THE IMAGE OF THE TRIUNE GOD

As I mentioned a moment ago, God exists as three persons: Father, Son, and Holy Ghost. Man also exists as a triune reflection of God: body, soul, and spirit. The spirit is the part of us that communicates and cultivates our relationship with God. For example, when you pray in the spirit, your spirit is communicating directly with God. The soul consists of our will, intellect, and emotions. The body contains the spirit and the soul; it carries out the desires of the spirit or the soul and acts as our contact point with the material world.

Originally, Adam and Eve were guided by their spirits, and

because their spirits existed in an unhindered relationship with God, they lived devoid of sin. But when sin entered through Adam and Eve, a stake was driven through their spirits, leaving the soul in charge, and the body became the instrument of the soul. Our soul (self-will, intellect, and emotions), in cooperation with our body and sinful nature, results in what the Bible calls *living by the flesh*. The society in which we live reflects a fallen world and fleshly living: crime, violence, sexual immorality, sickness, disease, and tragedy.

> Therefore, brethren, we are debtors, not to the flesh, to live after the flesh. For if ye live after the flesh, ye shall die: but if ye through the Spirit do mortify the deeds of the body, ye shall live. (Rom. 8:12–13)

When we give our lives to Jesus Christ, God breathes life into our spirits. As we exercise our spirits through prayer, reading the Word of God and acting in obedience, our spirit begins to grow. And the more our spirit grows, the more we are empowered to live as sons and daughters of Perez. If, however, we don't feed and exercise our spirits, we become spiritually stunted.

WHETHER WE'RE GODLY OR UNGODLY, THE PRINCIPLES OF DOMINION AND AGREEMENT ARE STILL AT WORK

God's original plan at creation was for man to be led by His Spirit. It was in this state of spiritual oneness with God that man was given dominion over the earth. Through man, God would then accomplish His will on this earth. Unfortunately, as we all know, Adam and Eve didn't abide by this plan:

> And the LORD God said, Behold, the man is become as one of us,
> to know good and evil: and now, lest he put forth his hand, and
> take also of the tree of life, and eat, and live for ever. (Gen. 3:22)

At the point that Adam and Eve sinned, their spirits became dormant and God lost His partners in accomplishing His will. However, two principles were still at work: man's dominion and the power of agreement. By the time we get to Genesis 11, it quickly becomes apparent that mankind took these two principles to heart.

> And the LORD said, Behold, the people is one, and they have all
> one language; and this they begin to do: and now nothing will be
> restrained from them, which they have imagined to do. Go to, let
> us go down, and there confound their language, that they may
> not understand one another's speech. (Gen. 11:6–7)

The people were one in speech and one in purpose, but they weren't one with God. Even in their fallen state, they imitated their Creator and joined together in agreement to build a great tower to the heavens. Their goal was to take dominion.

God's original plan of perpetrating *His* purposes through mankind was perverted into an exercise in self-glorification. So God said, "If I don't stop them, they'll accomplish whatever they have a heart and a mind to do." Then He thrust different languages upon them and scattered them throughout the earth.

Directly following this episode, God propelled into motion His plan to redeem the world and raise up a people who would join Him in accomplishing His will on the earth. In Genesis 12 we are introduced to a great man of faith named Abram (later renamed Abraham) whom God promised, "I will make of thee a great nation, and I will bless thee, and make thy name great; and thou shalt be a blessing . . . and in thee shall all families of the earth be blessed" (Gen. 12:2–3). Through Abraham and Abraham's seed, God would send Jesus, the Son of God and the Prince of breakers, and He would anoint His people to establish God's purposes here on earth.

GOD IS SEARCHING FOR A PEOPLE TO JOIN HIM IN AGREEMENT

As you can see, since the beginning of creation God has been looking for a people who would simply join Him in agreement. And when we finally come to our senses and meet God's clarion call for a partner, there will be loosed a power within us the likes of which this world has never witnessed.

When God does find that person or group, the devil will do anything in his power to divide them. He will try to set their minds in disagreement with their bodies and their spirits in disagreement with their minds. Satan wants us confused so he can neutralize the one human entity equipped to overpower him.

Now is the time for us, the church, to realize that we are made in the image of God and have already been given dominion over all the earth. We were created to perpetrate God's will here on earth. The reason why sickness and disease are present isn't because God allows them. Sickness and disease are present because *we* allow them. Sickness and disease are present because we have allowed Satan to neutralize the people of God.

GOD'S WORD NEVER RETURNS VOID BECAUSE HE IS BOUND BY HIS WORD

Jesus said that His followers would lay hands on the sick and they would recover (see Mark 16:18). He promised that His followers would do greater works than He would do (see John 14:12). If God says He will do something, He is bound by His word to do it. God spoke through the prophet Ezekiel, "For I am the LORD: I will speak, and the word that I shall speak shall come to pass" (Ezek. 12:25). In a world of broken promises, we can be confident that God honors His promises. Every one of them!

The fulfillment of God's promises, however, is not immediate. In the book of Isaiah God explains:

> For as the rain cometh down, and the snow from heaven, and returneth not thither, but watereth the earth, and maketh it bring forth and bud, that it may give seed to the sower, and bread to the eater: So shall my word be that goeth forth out of my mouth: it shall not return unto me void, but it shall accomplish that which I please, and it shall prosper in the thing whereto I sent it. (Isa. 55:10–11)

This text presents one of the greatest paradoxical statements in the entirety of holy writ. At the beginning the passage reads, "My word . . . returns not thither." But immediately following it the text reads, "My word that returns unto me." How can God's word return and not return at the same time? It seems to be a contradiction.

GOD SENDS HIS WORD . . .

The key to understanding this passage lies in distinguishing *who* is doing *what*. God sends His word. In Psalm 107:20, God speaks through the psalmist: "He sent his word, and healed them, and delivered them from their destructions." God has already sent His Word. We call it the Bible.

But if simply having the Word of God in our hands were enough to heal people, all you would need to do is lay your Bible on a cancer patient, and that patient would be made well. But doing so would yield the same result as laying a copy of *Reader's Digest* on the same person. Something, or better yet, Someone, is missing.

. . . WE RETURN IT TO GOD

God's Word is like dynamite that is planted in the ground. It's full of power, but somebody still has to flip the switch. God sends His Word, but it is our responsibility to place it within our humanity because our humanity is where our authority is housed. Remember that God gave mankind dominion, which means to dominate or rule.

God sent His Word and He gave us the authority to enforce it. Where there's sickness, we can heal. Where there is brokenness, we can restore. Where there is hopelessness, we can bring hope. Where there is sorrow, joy. Where there is mourning, gladness. So how do we do it?

THE SECRET OF THE POWER OF THE HOLY SPIRIT

Here is the secret to moving in the power of the Holy Spirit: Jesus said in John 7:38, "He that believeth on me, as the scripture hath said, out of his belly shall flow rivers of living water."

What is water a symbol of in Scripture? The Holy Spirit. In other words, out of our bellies will flow rivers (notice that it's plural, meaning an overabundance) of the Holy Ghost.

The phrase "out of our bellies" is not entirely accurate. The word for "belly" can also be translated "innermost part," or better yet, "womb."[2]

For all intents and purposes, a womb is a generator. It takes one form of energy and through process releases that energy into another form. If you work on a construction site and there's no electricity to run your saw, you get yourself a generator, pour some gasoline into it, turn it on, and electricity comes out.

Our spirit works the same way. We begin by ingesting the Word of God into our belly, our innermost part—our spiritual generator. And watch what comes out:

> This book of the law shall not depart out of thy mouth; but thou shalt meditate therein day and night, that thou mayest observe to do according to all that is written therein: *for then thou shalt make thy way prosperous, and then thou shalt have good success.* (Josh. 1:8, italics added)

> My son, attend to my words; incline thine ear unto my sayings. Let them not depart from thine eyes; keep them in the midst of thine heart. *For they are life unto those that find them, and health to all their flesh.* (Prov. 4:20–22, italics added)

> Thy word have I hid in mine heart, *that I might not sin against thee.* (Ps. 119:11, italics added)

Notice that these Scriptures don't apply just to wealth and physical healing. They also apply to the sinful, fleshly appetites that so easily govern our lives. By feeding our spirits with the Word of God, we counteract the power of sin. The Word of God is truly the sword that enables us to cut through the bondages of any problem that stands between us and the will of God. The sword of the Spirit is a powerful weapon in the hands of a breaker!

This principle is vitally important because it may save your life, your children, and even your marriage.

THE SEED OF GOD'S WORD
MUST DIE WITHIN YOU

Your body may be full of pain, but God has already sent His Word, and your responsibility is to drop the seed of that Word into the fertile soil of your human spirit. Once it is planted there, the seed goes through a process of death. "Unless a kernel of wheat falls to the ground and dies, it remains only a single seed. But if it dies, it produces many seeds" (John 12:24 NIV).

The Word has to die in you. What does that mean? It becomes a part of you. You believe God's Word more than you believe what your eyes see or your ears hear. When the doctor says there's something in your breast that shouldn't be there, you don't hang your head, because that Word has already died inside you.

The angel of God told John the Revelator, while he was on the island of Patmos, to *eat* that book (see Rev. 10:9). We need to ingest the Word of God because it goes in as food and comes out as energy. It needs to make such a spiritual transformation on the inside of us that we can't help but believe what it says.

But if you first get the doctor's report and then you go looking for your Bible, you've waited too long. The Word needs to die in you *first*.

You can't have what I'm talking about if you spend more time watching reruns on television than reading the Word. You have to be passionate about that Book. And the more you read it and meditate on it, the stronger your spirit will become until you're possessed by the Holy Spirit. Then you'll love reading your Bible more than watching talk shows or your favorite sports team.

As we feed on the Word of God, as we come into agreement with it and we let it die, the Breaker's power will bubble up within us with such great force that Satan will have no weapon to counter us. The time is now for this breaker generation to fill themselves up with the Word of God and then march forward to take back what we have allowed the devil to steal.

Armed with this knowledge, we can now become men and women of virtue, valor, vigor, and overpowering wealth.

PART II

VIRTUE:
THE CHARACTER OF
THE BREAKER

CHAPTER 4

THE POWER PRINCIPLE

The legacy we leave behind after passing through the portals of this mortal life says more about us than our opinions, pursuits, and plans. We take nothing with us to heaven, but we bequeath a legacy to those whose lives we touched—for good or for evil.

Legacy. It's a word that often surfaces in the course of conversation when remembering a person who has recently died. A legacy is an intangible trait or characteristic one leaves to the next generation. Some people leave a legacy of adultery that is passed on to their children and their children's children. Others leave a legacy of dishonesty. Far more rarely do people leave a legacy of righteousness.

Perez was a man who left an amazing legacy:

> All the sons of Perez that dwelt at Jerusalem were four hundred threescore and eight valiant men. (Neh. 11:6)

What is so amazing about this passage is that these 468 men were even known as the sons of Perez. *From the time of their forefather to the time of Nehemiah was almost fifteen hundred years!* Despite the information available through our advances in technology, no one today would be able to trace his ancestors back fifteen hundred years to A.D. 500. Out of the thirty-seven or thirty-eight generations separating Perez and Nehemiah, Perez left a legacy that distinguished him from his peers. One element that contributed to this breaker's legacy was virtue as witnessed in his descendents being selected to return with Nehemiah to Jerusalem.

Virtue is defined as "moral excellence and righteousness." A virtuous person lives above reproach regardless of whether someone is looking or not. But *virtue* can also be defined as "effective force or power," such as the virtue of prayer.[1] Virtue is the force of a righteous life that not only exposes the godly character of the breaker but also empowers it. Rather than adapt to the morals of the surrounding culture, a virtuous life adopts the unchanging precepts of a holy God.

YOU'RE SANCTIFIED *FROM* SOMETHING AND *TO* SOMETHING

> And the LORD spake unto Moses, saying, Speak unto the children of Israel, and say unto them, When either man or woman shall separate themselves to vow a vow of a Nazarite, to separate themselves unto the LORD . . . (Num. 6:1–3)

God called the children of Israel to live holy lives (see Lev. 19:1–2), but He also called a remnant of people to live at an even higher standard. These remnant people, the Nazirites, separated themselves unto the Lord. This act of separation, which we could also call consecration or sanctification, is usually perceived as a long list of don'ts. Most Christians believe that sanctification is separation *from* the world, and it is (see 2 Cor. 6:17). But you're not just sanctified *from* something, you're also sanctified *to* something, or better yet, Some*one*: God. In fact, the phrase "unto the Lord" is mentioned eight times in this chapter alone. We're sanctified to know God, to worship God, to obey God, to enjoy God.

Sanctification isn't just the eradication of sin, it is our dedication to God's purposes. And when we dedicate ourselves to pursuing God's purposes for our lives, we release God's power to move in our lives. That's why God's power is released in worship—because that's what we were created to do. That's why God gives us supernatural abilities in certain tasks—because that's what we were created to do.

If you find that you are skilled with your hands, then building homes or fixing cars may be part of God's purpose for your life—as you dedicate yourself to Him. In Exodus 31, God tells Moses to appoint Bezaleel and Aholiab to create the elements for the tabernacle. These are men who God says are filled "with the spirit of God, in wisdom, and in understanding, and in knowledge, and in all manner of workmanship" (Ex. 31:3). You don't have to be a pastor to be consecrated to God, you just need to be dedicated to His purposes.

But something interesting happens when we begin pursuing God's purposes for our lives: We try to avoid sin. When we know that we're in the middle of God's purposes and we see Him using us for His glory, we don't want to do anything to mess it up. True vision from God restrains sin.

PURITY RELEASES GOD'S POWER

Sanctification is not propelled only by purpose, but also by purity. That's why the Bible says to worship God in the beauty of holiness. "Give unto the LORD the glory due unto his name; worship the LORD in the beauty of holiness" (Ps. 29:2). What is holiness? Separation. Consecration. Dedication. What does God see as beautiful? Our purity.

No one ever stood on a pile of trash at a garbage dump and said, "What a beautiful sight!" But stand atop a mountain range as the sun slowly rises in the east, and what thoughts come to mind? Beauty, but also purity. And really, isn't that what beauty is? Just as a beautiful song or a picturesque landscape moves us, so our purity moves God. When we enter God's presence with clean hands, a pure heart, and dedication to His purposes, God's power is released.

> Who shall ascend into the hill of the LORD? or who shall stand in his holy place? He that hath clean hands, and a pure heart; who hath not lifted up his soul unto vanity, nor sworn deceitfully. He shall receive the blessing from the LORD, and righteousness from the God of his salvation. (Ps. 24:3–5)

Mount Sinai, the mountain of the Lord, was the place Moses encountered God in all His glory. In the same way, the mountain of the Lord for us is the manifest presence of God.

Sanctification, then, not only deals with what we do, but also with who we are. As Christians, we are made holy, but we are also in the process of becoming holy. Driving us forward into living sanctified lives are purpose and purity.

BEING A BREAKER IS A CHOICE WE MAKE

The rest of Numbers 6 explains the conduct of a person taking a Nazirite vow, which included:

- Avoiding contact with dead bodies

- Abstaining from wine and strong drink

- Allowing one's hair to grow without being cut

Then God spoke to Moses,

> This is the law of the Nazarite who hath vowed, and of his offering unto the LORD for his separation, beside that that his hand shall get: according to the vow which he vowed, so he must do after the law of his separation. (Num. 6:21)

God said, "This is the law of the Nazirite." He didn't say, "This is the law of every Israelite." There is a level of sanctification that deals with everybody, and then there is a level of sanctification that deals with people who want to go the extra mile in their walk with God. People who aren't content with life as they know it. People who want to *live* in the supernatural power of God. People with the heart of a breaker who are willing to mature beyond the letter of the law so that God anoints them with power.

There are certain things that God's Word has already told you to do. But there are other things, as you open your life, that God may call you to do that He may not call other people to do. Jesus told Peter, "Get out of the boat." But He didn't say it to John or the rest of the disciples.

BEING A BREAKER MEANS GOING BEYOND WHAT IS LEGALLY REQUIRED

Some people look at the way I live and ask, "Do you have to live that way?"

"No."

Or they ask me, "Do you have to do that to go to heaven?"

"No. What does that have to do with anything? Heaven is not all this world is about."

Everybody wants to operate in the supernatural power of God and experience the supernatural blessings of God while living in natural consecration. People assume that if they go to church every Sunday morning, pay their tithe, and remain faithful to their spouse, they're living extraordinary lives. But that's only living up to what God has required.

Something is wrong when we only go to church on Sunday morning in order to get church out of the way for the coming week. We call Sunday the Lord's Day, yet we treat going to church on Sunday night as an option. In fact, just by observing the practices of most Christians, you would think that we really observed only "the Lord's morning" because Sunday afternoon is reserved for watching sports on television and Sunday evening is spent catching up on whatever we procrastinated doing over the weekend.

According to a study conducted in 2000 by the Barna Group, born-again Christians are some of the most generous people in the world. In fact, the level of giving among born-again Christians is double the national average in the United States. However, twice as many born-again Christians *don't* give a dime to their churches throughout the year (16 percent) as those who tithe (only 8 percent). Even more disturbing in the Barna study is the discovery that the more money a person earns, the less likely he or she is to tithe.[2]

Christians are the most blessed people in the most blessed country in the world, and yet not even 10 percent tithe! And the greater the blessing, the less we give! Tithing has become the exception rather than the rule in our churches, even though God tells us that we are robbing Him when we fail to give Him what is rightfully His–the tithe (see Mal. 3:8).

Jesus said that when a man looks lustfully at a woman, he has already committed adultery in his heart. Yet many Christian men see no problem with flipping through the swimsuit edition of their favorite magazine. Never before has pornography been so readily available to so many people, and never before have so many people been enslaved by it. Our churches *and* our church leaders struggle with it to the same extent as the world. Somehow we've convinced ourselves that it's okay to look as long as we don't touch. But how can God bless us when we can't even live within what is required?

WE WANT HEAVEN'S PRIVILEGES
AT HELL'S PRICES

Although I don't look at the giving records at my church, people from our accounting department tell me that one week a person will give $100.02 and the next week the same person will give $100.03. Then the next week $100.02 and then the next week $100.03. People like this can't split the penny, so they have to give one the first week and then leave it out the next, and so on. People like this are only trying give what is legally required.

But being a breaker means going beyond what is legally required. We commit ourselves to the life of our church, we cheerfully give our tithes *and* offerings, and we live our lives above reproach whether or not anyone is watching.

Stop doing the minimum and sell out! We want Peter's power and John's authority at hell's prices. But these men left their jobs and occasionally left their families for years at a time. Tradition holds that Peter was martyred while hanging upside down on a cross, and John was unsuccessfully boiled in a vat of hot oil. Jacob wrestled the angel of the Lord all night for a blessing that he received—he became the father of the twelve tribes of Israel. But he also walked away from the ordeal with a limp that stayed with him the rest of his life.

If you want the Lord to bless you, if your kids are sick or your spouse is depressed, if you're having trouble in your finances, then you have to go beyond the ordinary.

THE GREATER THE CONSECRATION, THE GREATER THE ANOINTING

We need to be people who ask, "How far from the world can I get and still be effective on this earth?" rather than, "How close to hell can I live and still squeeze into heaven?"

But when we finally decide to sell out, we're going to experience such a great outpouring of power that everything we're experiencing now is going to look like a Sunday school picnic. The power of God is going to come, and we're not even going to have to pray for people to get out of their wheelchairs. They won't have any choice but to get up because the power of God will be so strong.

You see, sanctification is a power principle. The more consecrated we are, the more of the anointing we experience.

God told me long ago, "You can have as much of Me as you are willing to pay for. But I don't come cheap." Salvation is a gift from God that we do nothing to earn. But sanctification, and the power that follows, carries a price. For instance, Joshua told the people of Israel, "Sanctify yourselves: for to morrow the LORD will do wonders among you" (3:5).

Sometimes people see someone who is anointed and say to themselves, *Oh, I wish I were anointed like that.* But I don't believe them; I don't think they are willing to do what it takes to walk in that kind of anointing. Do you know why we don't perform the works that Jesus did? Because we aren't willing to do what Jesus did. We don't consecrate ourselves completely unto the Lord.

SANCTIFICATION MEANS LIVING A FASTED LIFE

But to move into deeper levels of anointing requires spiritual maturity. There are certain areas in my life that God has asked me to give up. They weren't sins in themselves, but God asked me to go without them. So I did. For ten years at a time God has instructed me, "Don't eat this anymore" or "Don't drink that anymore." And I didn't because I want as much of God in my life as possible.

Then suddenly, He lifted His hand and said, "Well, that's all right now. You can have it back."

We have to be careful that we don't become legalistic by requiring of others what God is requiring only of us or requiring of us what God is requiring only of others. But as you seek after God with your whole heart and commit yourself to following in obedience, He'll reveal it to you.

When most people hear the term *fasting*, they think of going without food for long periods of time—as long as forty days. But God doesn't expect you to fast only from food in order to walk in a greater anointing. It's one way, but not the only way.

The Nazirites weren't required to go on a forty-day fast from all food. But they were instructed to refrain from wine and grapes, and they were commanded not to cut their hair or touch dead bodies. *The Nazirites lived a fasted lifestyle.*

Living a fasted lifestyle means avoiding those things God has forbidden you to touch. There should be things other people do that you don't do. There should be things other families do that your family doesn't do. You may be going to a certain place regularly and suddenly you stop going there. Not because there's anything wrong with going there, but just because you gave it up for God— it may be a food, it may be something you drink, it may be a hobby, it may even be television.

Why do you do it? Because you prayed, "Lord, I want to get rid of any stuff that might come between You and me. I don't have to live like this crazy bunch of worldlings; I sanctify this unto You until You remove Your hand from it."

When we're in tune with the Spirit, there is always something God is putting His hand on that He wants us to give to Him. I gladly live a fasted lifestyle because I don't want to just go to heaven. I want the power of God.

WHERE'S THE POWER?

God's not trying to get you to be holy just so He can make you march around like some kind of little wooden soldier in obedience to Him. He's trying to get you power. He said, "Be holy as I am holy." He said, "Do you want to be powerful as I am powerful? Do you want to have dominion as I have dominion? Then sanctify yourself."

Why do we hear so few voices crying out, "Where's the power?" Why do we have to have fourteen people laying hands on someone just to get a little bit of the blessing from God into their lives?

We should be able to walk down the street and people will get healed because our shadows touch them. A tangible anointing of God should rest so greatly upon us that we can walk through the grocery store and people in the aisle across from us are convicted of sin. In this end-time hour, God will use us to do these things as we begin to set ourselves apart through a sanctified life.

THE GLORY OF A SANCTIFIED LIFE

When a Nazirite vow was completed, the person was given explicit instructions on how to bring it to an end. One interesting element involved the hair of the person making the vow. Have you ever wondered why people taking a Nazirite vow, like Samson, were supposed to keep their hair long? Here is why:

> And the Nazarite shall shave the head of his separation at the door of the tabernacle of the congregation, and shall take the hair of the head of his separation, and put it in the fire which *is* under the sacrifice of the peace offerings. (Num. 6:18)

At the conclusion of the vow, the person was to stand at the entrance of the tabernacle, shave his or her hair, and then walk forward to burn it on the brazen altar. Throughout the vow, the person's hair grew for a specific purpose: to be burned on the altar.

Hair represents a person's glory. This was as true then as it is now. Some people spend hours primping, curling, and combing their hair. When it isn't fashioned just right, we say we're having a "bad hair day." We spend all that time on our hair because that is what people see. It brings glory to us. But the person taking the Nazirite vow understood that his or her vow was intended to bring glory to God.

The breaker who lives a virtuous life understands that his or her sanctified life is not intended to impress people, but to bring glory to God. To live a life of purity and purpose in order to be a conduit of God's power and glory. And most of all, to please God.

WE SANCTIFY OURSELVES
BECAUSE WE LOVE HIM

Imagine for a moment walking into your child's room early one morning (assuming you have a child) to find the bed made, the furniture dusted, and the room completely clean—and you didn't even have to tell your child to do it! Then, while trying to catch your breath, your child runs up to you, gives you a big hug and says, "I just want you to know I love you and I appreciate your letting me live here. You didn't have to do it."

Apart from feeling chest pains from the shock, you would probably feel appreciated, and you would likely reward your child with something special.

That's what God is like. He didn't have to send Jesus to die on an old rugged cross for us. He didn't have to heal us. He didn't have to deliver us. He didn't have to wake us up this morning.

Nothing warms the heart of our heavenly Father more than to hear us say, "You didn't have to do what You've done for me, so to show You how much I appreciate it, I commit myself to living beyond what You require. Not because I have to, but because I want to. Because I love You."

How does God respond? As any good father would. He wraps His powerful arms around us and shares with us the full extent of His love.

CHAPTER 5

THE BRIDGE FROM
BONDAGE TO BLESSING

They had spent their entire lives enduring the arid heat of the Sinai desert. A nomadic existence wasn't exactly their lifestyle of choice, but they persevered knowing that once God felt they were ready, they would move into the promised land. The only thing worse than sitting in the desert for forty years was living in slavery to the Egyptians as their parents had. Or so they thought.

The slavery their parents experienced was oppressive, and being treated like animals gave them an appreciation for human life. But God raised up a man by the name of Moses who delivered them from the Egyptians. When Pharaoh released them, the people were beside themselves. Every time they faced an obstacle crossing the desert, God provided a way through, usually at the last minute. At one point, Pharaoh changed his mind and sent his massive army to bring the Israelites back into bondage, cornering them against the Red Sea. But God parted the waters and the people crossed the sea on dry ground. When the Egyptians followed in after them, the waters closed, swallowing the entire army.

All that stood, then, between their parents and the promised land was sand, the Jordan River . . . and themselves. Whenever a problem surfaced, such as not having any food, the people complained to Moses and begged to go back to Egypt. While Moses was on Mount Sinai receiving instruction from God for the people, the people complained and rebelled against Moses and God. When Moses came down the mountain and saw the people worshiping idols and indulging in orgies, he was irate. But if not for Moses' pleading on behalf of the Israelites, God would have destroyed the people right there. God and Moses disciplined them severely to teach them that they were called to a higher standard than that of the surrounding nations.

Despite the mighty acts and God continually working on their behalf, the rebellion and grumbling continued. When they finally reached the Jordan River, Moses sent twelve spies across to assess what would be required to possess the promised land. But ten of the twelve reports weren't very promising. The land God had promised *was* truly the land of milk and honey. The soil was fertile for crops; the grass was good for their herds of cattle and sheep. But there was one *big* obstacle: The inhabitants were huge!

Fear gripped the people. Again some demanded to go back to Egypt. Others started a revolt against their leader. And once again Moses was placed in the unenviable position of convincing God not to destroy His chosen people. "The people aren't ready to enter into My promise," God told Moses. "There is still too much Egypt in Israel." For the next forty years Israel waited in the desert for a generation to die and another one to grow up that would understand what it means to live as God's chosen people.

OBEDIENCE IS THE BRIDGE FROM BONDAGE TO BLESSING

Forty years later the people stood on the banks of the Jordan River, ready to take possession of the land and enter God's blessing. Moses was now gone and Joshua had assumed his mantle of leadership. But before crossing, Joshua told the people, "Wait. Before we cross the river, we need to consecrate ourselves to God" (see Josh. 3:5).

Fifteen hundred years later, just before He ascended into heaven, Jesus instructed His fledgling church to tarry in Jerusalem; to wait for the gift of the Holy Spirit. And fifty days later, on Pentecost Sunday, the Holy Spirit was poured out on all flesh, Jerusalem was turned upside down, and the world has never been the same.

Two thousand years later, history has repeated itself and the church once again sits on this side of their spiritual Jordan, waiting to enter the blessing of God's promised land. We have the promise, but like the children of Israel in the wilderness, we've chosen bondage over blessing. We've rebelled against our leaders and our God. We complain and grumble about the troubles we've brought upon ourselves. And God says, "You aren't ready. You need to consecrate yourselves and choose once again whom you will serve."

There's a step between bondage and blessing. People want to bypass the middle step because it requires perseverance. What is that step? It is obedience. It is the bridge that takes us from bondage to blessing.

GOD CALLS US TO CROSS WHEN OUR JORDAN IS HIGHEST AND THE CHALLENGE IS GREATEST

After consecrating themselves to the Lord that day, the people gathered their things the next morning and faced the Jordan. The river at this time of the year wasn't a little meandering stream. It was overflowing its banks. Imagine trying to safely transport an entire nation of people across a river overflowing its banks without losing any lives. With human strength alone, it would be impossible. But the God of the supernatural promised to part the river.

When God calls us to obey, He usually waits until our situation looks impossible: a lost job, a terminal illness, a child on drugs. Just about anyone can step out in obedience when faith isn't required and all the signs in the natural point to success. But you can hardly consider it obedience if it doesn't cost you something.

When the children of Israel woke up the morning they were to cross the Jordan, the waters weren't already parted, waiting for them to walk through. When the people stood up to cross the river, the banks were still overflowing. It wasn't until the priests leading the group stepped into the waters that the river began to recede.

OBEDIENCE IS ALSO A POWER PRINCIPLE

In the last chapter, I explained that sanctification is a power principle. As we consecrate ourselves to God and remove anything that stands in the way of our relationship with Him, power is released in our lives. But obedience is also a power principle. God's miracle-working power is released when we obey.

When Jesus was attending a wedding in Cana, the bridal party ran out of wine. In the culture of that time, running out of any supplies at a wedding would have been a great disgrace. Wedding celebrations lasted for a week, and the hosts were expected to provide lavishly for their guests. But to run out of wine was a social no-no. Guests of the wedding party would joke about it for years. Then Jesus' mother, Mary, rounded up the servants, brought them to Jesus, and told them, "Whatever He says to you, do it. It doesn't matter if it doesn't make any sense; whatever He asks for, just give it to Him."

Jesus then asked for six stone jars that were used for ceremonial washing but forbidden by the Pharisees to hold drinking water. The servants brought them to Him, and He turned the water into wine.

The attitude that releases the power of God says, "God, I consecrate *everything* to You. If You want me to go somewhere, Lord, I'll go. If You *don't* want me to go somewhere, I won't go. If You ask it of me, I'll give up my front-row seat in church, I'll serve in the nursery, and I'll share Jesus with my neighbor."

GOD PUSHES US OUT OF OUR COMFORT ZONES FOR OUR OWN GOOD

If there isn't a divine disturbance going on in your life, you're probably tuned in to the wrong frequency. If He's not tearing down your scaffolding, then you're probably not where He wants you to be right now. God is in the business of ruffling our feathers and pushing us out of the nest because He wants us to depend on no one but Him.

Once He pushes you over the edge, you feel as if you're in a free fall, flopping and floundering, because He's teaching you to fly. Although you're falling, you certainly aren't failing. Then, at the last possible moment, just before you crash, He swoops down and rescues you.

But that's not the end of it. He carries you back to your nest only to repeat the exhilarating experience on another day. He's exercising your faith so that you can soar at greater levels of obedience and become the breaker He created you to be.

OUR ACTS OF OBEDIENCE GO FROM THE HARDEST TO THE EASIEST

The priests of Israel stepped into the Jordan River, the waters parted, and the people walked across on dry land, just as they had with Moses at the Red Sea. But their test of faith was far from over. Facing them when they crossed the river was the greatest opposition they would encounter.

Five miles ahead stood Jericho, the great walled city. With the enormous number of people crossing the Jordan, the people in Jericho undoubtedly heard the commotion. God didn't bring the Israelites farther downstream where no one would see them. He brought them across where Israel would face the greatest enemy of their thirty-one conquests and where their greatest enemy would witness an entire nation crossing the Jordan on dry land.

When God requires acts of obedience, He doesn't start with the easiest and work to the hardest. He always starts out with the hardest and works toward the easiest. Don't think you have to fight this little devil, and then that little devil, and then another little devil. God wants you to conquer the big one first so that all the smaller ones get scared and scamper off.

PERVERTING GOD'S PURPOSES BRINGS A CURSE

Jericho became the test to see how obedient the Israelites really were. The people obeyed Joshua's instructions and marched around Jericho in silence once a day for six days. On the seventh day, they marched around the walled fortress six times and before the seventh time, Joshua gave them these strict instructions:

> And ye, in any wise keep yourselves from the accursed thing, lest ye make yourselves accursed, when ye take of the accursed thing, and make the camp of Israel a curse, and trouble it. (Josh. 6:18)

Notice one particular word He used: *accursed.* Joshua said you can touch certain things that will curse you. The Hebrew word for *accursed* literally means "devoted."[1] When we take what is devoted to God and pervert it for our own use, it becomes a curse. But God isn't the one who sends it.

Any time we pervert God's purposes, we bring a curse upon ourselves.

- Why are fornication and homosexuality sins? Because God intended all sexual relationships to be shared between one man and one woman in a covenant relationship with Him.

- Why is greed a sin? Because God intended to bless us so that we would bless others and finance the spread of the gospel.

- Why is lying a sin? Because it is a perversion of the truth.

In order for something to be perverted, it must begin as something good. Evil cannot become perverted because it already *is* perverted. In this case, God's instructions to Israel dealt with finances and material possessions:

> But all the silver, and gold, and vessels of brass and iron, are consecrated unto the LORD: they shall come into the treasury of the LORD. (Josh. 6:19)

Upon conquering Jericho, Israel was instructed not to keep any of the plunder to themselves. Just as we give the firstfruits of our tithe to God, the Israelites were instructed to give the entire plunder of their first conquest to God. After this initial victory, the people would then be able to keep the plunder.

Notice that what God calls "accursed" in verse 18 He calls "consecrated" in verse 19. What we do with what God gives us determines which is which.

OUR SANCTIFICATION, OR LACK OF IT, AFFECTS THE WHOLE CHURCH

> But the Israelites acted unfaithfully in regard to the devoted things; Achan son of Carmi, the son of Zimri, the son of Zerah, of the tribe of Judah, took some of them. So the LORD's anger burned against Israel. (Josh. 7:1 NIV)

Achan took what was devoted to God and used it for his own purposes. Did Israel obey God's command? If you consider that only one man out of Israel's massive army disobeyed—perhaps .00285 percent of the total—you would think that God would be satisfied. But He wasn't. God held the whole nation of Israel responsible for the sin of one man. This passage says, "The LORD's anger burned against *Israel.*"

A single, simple act of selfless obedience would have brought the anointing, but instead the disobedience of one made the entire nation accursed.

If we think the sins we commit behind closed doors affect no one else, we're only fooling ourselves. The reason our churches lack power is because our churches aren't *wholly* committed to living righteous lives. Never was the saying so true that the church is "only as strong as its weakest link."

OUR SANCTIFICATION, OR LACK OF IT, AFFECTS THE LOST AND DYING

There's a world of people out there who are damaged, depressed, diseased, and dying. They're lost and they can't find their way through the darkness.

They're hidden in crags of rock and underneath great pillars. In fear and trembling, they're trying to hide from God, and they don't know where to turn. They don't know who to turn to. And so they look to the church, but they find no power.

No one knew what had been committed in secret until Israel's next encounter with the Canaanites. The armies of Israel went into battle against a puny city named Ai and were soundly defeated. They went from defeating their greatest enemy to being defeated by their weakest enemy. "What happened to the power?" the people inquired of God.

Unfortunately, many churches lose their power but never ask what happened. They go through the same motions and they either ignore the defeat or they find new ways to explain the defeats they repeatedly encounter:

- "Well, the Spirit of God just isn't moving today as He did thirty years ago."

- "John may be dying of cancer, but he's healed in the spiritual; the natural just hasn't manifested itself yet."

- "I know we're not winning people to Christ right now, but God is calling us to focus on deepening our walk with Him."

WE NEED TO EMULATE JESUS, NOT THE WORLD

People are dying and going to hell because we aren't living in obedience to God. We're more concerned about our social status in the world than reflecting the character of Jesus.

The world has infected the church, our preaching, our music, our attitudes, even the way we do business. The other day I turned on the television and saw a girl singing who shocked me. She had three rings in her nose, spiked hair in three different colors, tattoos all over her arms, and her lip was pierced. "Dear God," I prayed, "what is that devil on my TV?" Then I realized I was watching a Christian station! And I thought to myself, *This is who we are telling young people to emulate?*

When people see someone with a big gold thing hanging out of their mouth, do they say to themselves, *Praise the Lord! That man must love the Lord with all of his heart!?* Who are we striving to be like?

When the world looks at the men and women in our churches, they should see Christians. The young ladies in my church look up to my wife and my mother because they carry themselves with dignity and when they lay hands on the sick, they get well. We need to look up to people because of the character, godliness, and power of God in their lives.

WE MUST BE WILLING TO GIVE UP ANYTHING AND EVERYTHING

Emulating the world means taking on the characteristics of the world. Emulating Jesus means growing in the character of Jesus and following in His footsteps by modeling complete obedience.

As Alexander the Great continued his conquest of the known world, he encountered a walled city that seemed impossible to conquer with the small contingent of soldiers that were traveling with him at the time. Standing outside the fortress, Alexander yelled out, demanding to see the king. After a few moments the king leaned over the wall.

"Surrender your city!" Alexander shouted to the king.

"Surrender?!?" the king replied. "Why should I surrender to you? Your small troop of men can't harm us."

"Watch," Alexander responded as he lined up his men. The townspeople leaned over the side of the wall to see what Alexander was doing. Once the men were in order, he took a deep breath and yelled, "March!"

Forward the men marched. The townspeople could see the edge of a cliff in the distance, but they were certain Alexander would stop them. But he didn't. One man, then another, then another marched off the edge of the cliff to a painful death. Finally, after ten men had fallen to their deaths, the king yelled, "Halt." The men stopped but continued facing forward.

"That is why you should surrender," the great leader calmly told the king. The people immediately opened the doors to the city and surrendered. They knew if the soldiers' allegiance to their commander was greater than their fear of death, nothing would keep them from victory.

Was Alexander the Great powerful? Yes. He was powerful because his soldiers were obedient even to the point of death.

The apostle Paul writes,

> Let this mind be in you, which was also in Christ Jesus: Who, being in the form of God, thought it not robbery to be equal with God: But made himself of no reputation, and took upon him the form of a servant, and was made in the likeness of men: And being found in fashion as a man, he humbled himself, and *became obedient unto death, even the death of the cross.* (Phil. 2:5–8, italics added)

In the same way that Jesus was obedient unto death, we are called to become obedient unto death. But when we respond in complete obedience, the power of God is released, bringing the victory over any weapon that is formed against us.

SOMETIMES WE'RE CALLED TO DO SOMETHING THAT MAKES NO SENSE

Sometimes God requires us to do some pretty crazy things that make no sense at all. He may tell you to sell your house and move into an apartment so you can concentrate on seeking His face. He may tell you to stop talking for a month, as He once told me. He may even tell you to enroll at a Bible college when you already have a Ph.D.

We don't always understand why He calls us to do what He calls us to do, but our responsibility is to obey first and ask questions later. Part of living a fasted lifestyle, as I explained in the last chapter, may mean acting in obedience on something that you won't understand for years down the road.

God once told me to give up a certain kind of food. Was there anything wrong with eating it? No. He just said, "Don't eat it." So I didn't.

For several years it went on. Then when my son Austin was diagnosed with Asperger's syndrome, the doctor explained that because of the way his brain functioned, he was locked in to eating specific kinds of foods.

God then spoke to me, "You didn't know it, but that's why I told you to give up that food two years ago. I gave you a two-year head start to sanctify yourself so you would have the power in your life to bring deliverance over that problem in your son's life." Shortly afterward, we began to experience a breakthrough in Austin's eating habits.

For two years I obeyed God without understanding why He was calling me to do it. You may go the rest of your life without understanding why He calls you to do something. And you know what that's called? Faith.

To this day I still don't touch that food. We've seen incredible breakthroughs in my son's life, but God said, "Once he gets his manifestation completely, then you're free to do whatever you want with that food."

Can I be honest with you? At times my flesh fights what God told me to do, but it cannot be compared with the glory and power that are released into my life. And the same can be true for you if you have the spirit of the breaker.

CHAPTER 6

WHOLLY HOLY
GHOST POSSESSED

In the last chapter we learned that obedience is the bridge from bondage to blessing. Because of the disobedience of only one man, the massive army of Israel was soundly defeated by the minute, insignificant army of Ai.

When the discouraged troops returned to their families, Joshua and the people were distraught. "God, how could this happen? Why would You lead us into the wilderness for forty years and then abandon us at the hands of this little village? We're the laughingstock of Canaan, and so are You!"

God then spoke to Joshua, "The reason why your troops lost the battle to Ai is because they first lost the battle to sin. There is sin in the camp." And then God said,

> Up, sanctify the people, and say, *Sanctify yourselves* against tomorrow. (Josh. 7:13, italics added)

Before God would move among His people once again, they would first have to sanctify themselves. Often in Scripture this was the pattern that prepared the people for God to move on their behalf.

When Israel was wandering in the wilderness and the people were complaining because they hadn't eaten meat since they left Egypt, God told them, "Sanctify yourselves against tomorrow, and ye shall eat flesh" (Num. 11:18). The next day God rained so many quail on the people that they eventually grew sick of eating it.

Just before crossing the Jordan and defeating Jericho, God commanded them, "Sanctify yourselves: for tomorrow the LORD will do wonders among you" (Josh. 3:5). The next day they crossed the Jordan, and a week later they stood and watched God tear down the walls of Jericho.

When Samuel was evaluating the sons of Jesse to determine who would be the next king of Israel, he first told the family, "Sanctify yourselves" (1 Sam. 16:5). Then God spoke to Samuel and said that the least likely son—David—would become the greatest king in Israel's history.

Sanctifying ourselves—intentionally setting ourselves apart to God—releases the power of God to instruct and intervene in our lives.

PRESENT YOURSELVES A LIVING SACRIFICE

Sanctifying ourselves is not just an old covenant command. In the New Testament, the apostle Paul expresses it this way:

> I beseech you therefore, brethren, by the mercies of God, that ye present your bodies a living sacrifice, holy, acceptable unto God, which is your reasonable service. And be not conformed to this world: but be ye transformed by the renewing of your mind, that ye may prove what is that good, and acceptable, and perfect, will of God. (Rom. 12:1–2)

Who is the apostle Paul speaking to? He is speaking to all of us. Seven times in these two verses he writes "you," "ye," or "your." The word *you* in the original language isn't singular but plural, meaning "you all." In other words, it's not our decision whether or not to offer ourselves as living sacrifices because God commands it of all of us.

Let me also say that sanctification is not legalism. The Bible asks all of us, "Who art thou that judgest another?" (James 4:12). Growing in sanctification is not a license to judge another person. If your mentality begins going that direction, then you miss the most important direction of all—the direction the Holy Spirit is taking *you*. Your level of sanctification is between God and you.

GOD'S RESPONSIBILITY: OUR POSITIONAL AND ULTIMATE SANCTIFICATION

Romans 12:1–2 deals with one of the three stages of sanctification. If you're a student of God's Word, you know that certain numbers are more significant than others in Scripture. The number three, for example, is the number for God and divine completeness:

- Jesus rose from the grave on the third day.

- The Father, Son, and Holy Ghost comprise the Trinity (which literally means "group of three").

- In the temple there's an outer court, an inner court, and the Holy of Holies.

- Originally, God ruled through three archangels: Michael, Lucifer, and Gabriel.

In the same manner, there are three stages of sanctification: positional, ultimate, and experiential. The first two are God's responsibility, and the last one is our responsibility.

Positional sanctification deals with our position in Christ. When you were born again, you received privileges and benefits you did nothing to deserve. You were made holy even though we all know that you aren't perfect. Ephesians 1 is a good example of what the Bible says about our positional sanctification. Reading that passage, we discover that God

- blessed us with all spiritual blessings in heavenly places in Christ (v. 3).

- chose us before the foundation of the world (v. 4).

- predestined us to be children of God (v. 5).

- redeemed us through the blood of His Son, Jesus (v. 7).

- abounded us with His wisdom and prudence (v. 8).

All these we receive by grace through faith in Christ Jesus. If you are in Christ, there is nothing you can do to receive any more of grace, and there is nothing you can do to have any less of it. It's all yours!

Ultimate sanctification is promised to those people who have already experienced positional sanctification. First John 3:2 tells us,

> Beloved, now are we the sons of God, and it doth not yet appear what we shall be: but we know that, when he shall appear, we shall be like him; for we shall see him as he is.

We struggle with sin in this mortal world, but someday sin will be defeated, Satan and his minions will be thrown into the lake of fire, and we will enjoy ultimate sanctification. We will see Christ and we will be like Christ. Sin will no longer be a struggle for us, and the effects of sin—sickness, disease, discouragement, and poverty—will be *completely* eliminated. And we will enjoy the presence of God forever.

But between our positional and ultimate sanctification is the fallen world in which we live.

OUR RESPONSIBILITY: EXPERIENTIAL SANCTIFICATION

The apostle Paul writes in 1 Corinthians 9:27, "I buffet my body and make it my slave, lest possibly, after I have preached to others, I myself should be disqualified" (NASB). Experiential sanctification is the process of buffeting our body and making it our slave while allowing the Holy Ghost to possess it and breathe His divine life into it.

Experiential sanctification can also be explained this way:

For if ye live after the flesh, ye shall die: but if ye through the Spirit do mortify the deeds of the body, ye shall live. (Rom. 8:13)

Allowing our flesh, our sinful nature, to lead our lives results in death. But through mortifying the deeds of our body, we will live. The word *mortify* literally means "to kill." There's nothing redemptive about our flesh. We're not supposed to feed it or suppress it or ignore it. The only thing we're supposed to do with it is kill it. The only good flesh is dead flesh.

Killing our flesh is only the first part. The passage continues,

For as many as are led by the Spirit of God, they are the sons of God. (Rom. 8:14)

We want to die to our flesh, but at the same time we want to be led by the Spirit, which is our heritage as the sons and daughters of

God. But only to the extent that we mortify the deeds of the flesh are we able to be led or possessed by the Spirit of God.

THE HOLY GHOST DEALS WITH EVERY PERSON DIFFERENTLY

Everything would be much easier if we had a big book of rules to follow, but we don't. Tapping into the power of the Breaker through experiential sanctification comes only through a living, up-to-date relationship with the Holy Ghost. It means allowing Him to constantly direct your thoughts, your actions, your attitudes, your desires, and your passions. When He says, "Do it," you do it. When He says, "Don't do it," you don't do it.

God has created every person differently and as a result, He deals with every person differently. The requirements for receiving eternal life remain the same, but God interacts differently with every person according to his or her gifts, abilities, personality, experiences, and so on. That's why we can't hold another person to the same measure of experiential sanctification that God holds us to.

Let me give you an example: There are many Christians who allow the world to creep into their lives through the magazines they read, the television shows they watch, and the music they listen to. God has given me limits regarding what I can allow to minister to my spirit.

But does that mean you're unsanctified if you ever read a secular magazine, watch a television show, or listen to music that isn't on the Christian radio station? No. What God speaks to one person may be different from what God speaks to another person, which may be quite different from what God speaks to you. You have to examine the fruit that it produces in your life, and you need anointed ears to hear what the Holy Ghost is speaking to you.

God might tell you, "Don't eat corn bread." If God told that to some people, they'd start a religion called "the corn-bread shunners." We need to loosen up a little bit about how God speaks to us and how He speaks to other people. We need to love God, love His truth, love His Word, love His people, seek His face, and then we won't be led astray. Let Him become your guide and your guard.

When you're in tune with the Holy Ghost, there are going to be some things He'll have you give up that are just between you and God. I don't eat certain foods for reasons that I haven't even shared with my wife. But God told me the day will come when I am going to be able to sit down and eat these foods, but not now. It's good to have some covenants just between you and God.

OUR CONFIDENCE COMES FROM A CLEAN CONSCIENCE

There are certain things that God allows me to do that He won't allow you to do. The Bible says, "If our heart"—which is our conscience—"condemn us not, then have we confidence toward God" (1 John 3:21). Our confidence before God comes from a clean conscience.

Trying to make people respond according to our conscience is a problem in many marriages. Sometimes the wife tries to be the conscience of her spouse. She tells him what is right and what is wrong. She says, "Do this," "Don't do that," "Are you sure that's the way God is leading you?" But she's not in his body and she's not the Holy Spirit. If you're married and you have some concerns about your spouse's conscience, often the best thing you can do is pray for him or her—that God would awaken your spouse's conscience. But don't try to play the Holy Spirit in your spouse's life!

Being sanctified doesn't mean you can walk up to a person in church and say, "My pastor said I should wear my sleeves to my knuckles; therefore I do and so should you." Being sanctified means wearing your sleeves the length the Holy Ghost tells you to wear them, in agreement with a clean conscience. Of course, there are things that the Holy Ghost would never tell you to do because He always agrees with the Word of God.

You can't make somebody else's word your word. When the disciples were on the boat in the Sea of Galilee and Jesus was walking on the water, He called only Peter to step out of the boat. He didn't tell James or John to join him. And the reason He didn't call any other disciples at that moment had nothing to do with their measure or lack of faith. He had His reasons for calling only Peter that may have had nothing to do with anyone else–except to bolster the faith of His disciples.

GOD IS TRYING TO ESTABLISH
WHO IS IN CHARGE

In order for us to be holy, we have to be wholly His. Completely. Being possessed by the Holy Ghost means if the Holy Ghost says, "I want you to go to church every morning to pray," then you go to church every morning and pray. If the Holy Ghost tells you, "Get up an hour early every morning and pray in tongues," then you get up an hour early every morning and pray in tongues.

We need to quit running around trying to obey some man-made list of rules. For eighteen years I didn't go to a movie theater because the Holy Ghost told me not to. But I never told anyone, "You better not be going to that movie house." Now don't get me wrong, I love to go to movies. A well-written, well-acted movie is *the* storytelling medium of our day, and I love a good story. But when the Holy Ghost said that to me, I never regretted not going to a movie because I knew that God knew what was best for me.

One day, however, my eight-year-old, Austin, crawled up on my lap—all ninety-five pounds of him—and said, "Daddy, I wouldn't be afraid to go to a movie, if you'd go with me." Now remember, God had told me to give up going to the movie theater. But at that point the Holy Ghost gave me a perfect peace that I should take him to a movie.

I could have been legalistic about it, but that's not what God is after. God is trying to establish who is in control. That was the issue when He called Abraham to offer his son Isaac on the altar on Mount Moriah. When the angel stopped him from slaying his son, Abraham could have been legalistic about it and said, "I don't care what the angel says, God told me to offer my son on the altar." Abraham could have killed his son and cut himself off from God's promised blessing. God was just testing Abraham to see where his heart was, and when he passed the test, God reaffirmed His promise of blessing (see Gen. 22).

That's how we need to live in the Holy Ghost. There may be times when you want to say something and you have the right to say something, but the Holy Ghost tells you, "Hold your tongue." He wants to see who is in control.

Once at the end of a church service, the Holy Ghost told me, "Go to the altar and pray." I obeyed and went forward. As I knelt down to pray, the people in my congregation started asking one another, "What's he doing?" Others tapped me on the shoulder asking, "What's the matter?"

"Nothing," I responded.

"Why are you at the altar?"

"Because God told me to pray."

Suddenly, everybody around me began crying. They thought something deep in the Spirit was taking place. But while on my knees I asked God, "Why did You have me come down here?" Then He answered me, "You can go back to your seat now. I just wanted to see if you would obey."

IT'S OBEDIENCE, NOT SACRIFICE,
THAT MOVES THE HAND OF GOD

It is not your sacrifice that moves the hand of God; it's your obedience. "To obey is better than sacrifice" (1 Sam. 15:22). There are other people more gifted than me who started a church the same time as me, but they're nowhere to be seen. What is important in the end is your obedience. God said, "Go," and I went. He said, "Stay," and I stayed. He said, "Say this," and I said it. He said, "Don't say that," and I shut my mouth.

How can God trust us to speak a word of life if He isn't Lord over our tongue? He cannot—and will not—use what He cannot control.

The difference between a wild horse and a trained horse is that a trained horse has been broken. A broken horse understands who is in charge and obeys. God's not about to jump on a wild horse and go for a Sunday ride. He's going to ride one that's been broken—one that understands who is in charge and obeys his Master's commands. God's not trying to break our spirit, but He is trying to get us to the point of having a submissive will so that He can guide us where we would never go on our own.

WE ARE GUIDED BY THE UNSEEN

Walking in the realm of the Spirit means we aren't guided by what we can see.

> Now faith is the substance of things hoped for, the evidence of things not seen. For by it the elders obtained a good report. Through faith we understand that the worlds were framed by the word of God, so that things which are seen were not made of things which do appear. (Heb. 11:1–3)

What would your life be like if you lived only by what you see? It wouldn't be any different than that of the majority of Christians. But the breaker lives by what he cannot see. He is guided by the invisible Holy Spirit, who creates something out of nothing. When you are possessed by the Holy Ghost, you become God's partner in establishing His invisible kingdom here on earth.

Walking by the Spirit can get some people really confused and uptight. "Well, I don't know whether it was God telling me to do that or the devil." As Christians we should be able to tell the difference between light and darkness. Jesus said, "And when he putteth forth his own sheep, he goeth before them, and the sheep follow him: *for they know his voice*" (John 10:4, italics added). If we know the Shepherd, then we should be able to recognize His voice. If you aren't able to discern God's voice on a regular basis, then I suggest you go back to Romans 8:13–14 and examine yourself to see if you need to mortify any deeds of the body.

Now let's review what we've learned so far: When dealing with the subject of sanctification, some Christians are permitted to say and do things that you can't say or do. On the other hand, you are permitted to say and do some things that other Christians aren't permitted to say and do.

But being led by the Spirit and focusing on what God says to *you* removes the splinter of judgmentalism that so often infects the body of Christ. "Judge not, that ye be not judged" (Matt. 7:1).

Learning to live by the Spirit, being possessed by the Holy Ghost, requires a commitment to progressive experiential sanctification. It means you're going to have to pray, read the Word, seek His face, discern His voice, walk in His statutes, love His truths, and embrace His commands. Nobody else can do it for you; you have to do it yourself. But being wholly Holy Ghost possessed empowers you with the Spirit of the Breaker to live above the world's standards and go beyond the powerless existence that so often plagues many believers.

PART III

VALOR:
THE COURAGE OF
THE BREAKER

CHAPTER 7

THE VALUE OF VALIANT
MEN AND WOMEN

We are privileged to witness a crucial moment in time when world events are converging with the fulfillment of Scripture. Those with the spiritual eyes to see can observe the consummation of the end of time. And those with the spiritual ears to hear can detect the approaching hoofbeats of the four horses of the apocalypse. The end of this world as we know may take place in our lifetime. Yet our churches are filled with a soft breed of Christians. The order of the day is fear rather than faith, comfort and convenience rather than commitment.

After all, the most excitement many experience is an occasional spaghetti dinner in the fellowship hall or a Saturday night bingo game because the church is busy reveling in its religion, ritualizing its praise and worship, and rejecting any resemblance of life. Many of our churches are nearly dead without the good sense to lie down. But they're going to have to die if they have any hope for living.

Our songs lack emotion. We manifest a mechanical gift, a memorized shout, a taught tongue, a learned dance. We can do the wave at the ballpark, but we're quick to criticize the brother who, with conviction in his heart, claps, dances, and shouts to the Lord with reckless abandonment. God forbid he ever run the aisles, for we will look down our religious nose at him and label him a "fanatic" and "out of control." Those who want more of God live in fear of those who are content with "church as usual."

We've traded righteousness and holiness for loose living and a corrupt conscience. Satan has subtly and systematically moved us from the realm of moral conservatism to the realm of moral liberalism. We have become well-versed in political policies rather than Bible basics and have sacrificed what is right on the altar of what is politically correct. Therefore, homosexuals are coming *out of* the closet while Christians are running *into* the closet because they don't want to clean *up* their closet.

Uncontrollable habits rather than an unceasing commitment to holiness rule our lives. We're living amid a generation whose passions lead us like riderless horses.

WE PROCLAIM A POWERLESS GOSPEL

Safely within the confines of our churches, we sing "Onward Christian Soldiers," but we live in fear of the world. What makes no sense to these self-contradictory people is that although they live in fear *of* the world, in many ways they're not different *from* the world. No wonder our spiritual and moral lives are so frail. I'm tired of being frail. I'm tired of making excuses. I'm tired of backing up. I'm tired of trying to explain our way out of it.

Such people can only be called weak adherents to a gospel they never really knew to begin with. These anemic men and women are strangers to the spirit of a breaker. They panic under pressure and create contagious and captivating fear.

We are raising a generation of men and women who are at the mercy of whatever life gives them. They serve a small God and, as a result, they live small lives. They've become content with sickness, disease, poverty, and powerlessness.

And so the world woefully exclaims, "Why would I want to be a part of this fraternity? They're obviously more miserable and living in more bondage than I am."

GOD IS RAISING UP A GENERATION OF VALIANT MEN AND WOMEN

As you are discovering in this book, there *is* a remnant of men and women who refuse to become a part of the religious institutions and orders that plague our society. They are the Samsons, the Samuels, the Davids, the Deborahs, the Esthers, and the Daniels of the present day.

Valiant men and women endowed with the spirit of the breaker understand that no matter what the circumstances are, no matter how bent their back may be, no matter how bloodied and bludgeoned their brow may become, no matter how staggering their steps may appear, no matter how rounded their shoulders may hang, there is a settled peace deep within their spirit saying, "I will rise up and live to fight another day."

These sons and daughters of Perez are not moved by society; rather, they are the movers and shakers of society who find a way to break through every line of Satan's defense. They are empowered with an ability to pass through, to pass over, to pursue, to overtake, and to recover all. They are infused with an ability and authority that are delegated from God Himself.

VALIANT MEN AND WOMEN ARE GOD'S MERCENARIES

After the wall surrounding Jerusalem was rebuilt by Nehemiah and his fellow Israelites, people volunteered to move back into the Holy City. Although the wall was finished, the safety of the city was far from secure. Jerusalem's inhabitants would need to be strong and courageous; they would need to be people who valued the defense of the city over their own lives.

The 468 sons of Perez who volunteered to resettle in Jerusalem are described in Nehemiah 11:6 as *valiant*, which means "mighty." But this term was also used to describe an elite warrior, like a modern-day Green Beret or Navy Seal. Referred to as "mighty men of valor," they were a social class who were respected for their military prowess.[1]

Any king worth his weight in shekels of gold surrounded himself with valiant men because he knew they would sacrifice their lives on his behalf. When a difficult mission was required, a man from the ranks of the mighty men of valor would bravely step forward to do what few others would even dream. Mighty men and women of valor are men and women of fearless courage. Their enemy is fear and their ally is faith in the God who gives them strength.

VALIANT MEN AND WOMEN REFUSE TO COWER IN THE PRESENCE OF A FORMIDABLE FOE

The fearful are unable to strike the strategic blow in the hour of conflict. But men who are possessed by the spirit of the breaker do not seek deliverance from the fires of adversity, nor do they petition the courts of heaven for responsibilities equal to their powers. Rather, they plead upon their knees for Holy Ghost power that is equal to their responsibility.

Like David, when facing their Goliath their confidence isn't based on their strengths, smarts, or skills. When the armies of Israel cowered in the presence of the Philistines and a formidable foe, only one man stood up to defend the reputation of his God. David knew what was required to face his greatest challenge. He needed a fearless courage that was grounded in his faith in God: "The LORD that delivered me out of the paw of the lion, and out of the paw of the bear, he will deliver me out of the hand of this Philistine" (1 Sam. 17:37).

With the armies of Israel and Philistia on either side, they watched a skinny, redheaded, freckle-faced, teenage boy face Goliath—a giant who had never known defeat. As Goliath raised his sword, David picked up his slingshot. But David didn't run from his enemy, he didn't stand and wait for his enemy; he pursued his enemy and defeated him.

These people are like Shadrach, Meshach, and Abednego, who refused to follow along with the crowd, even at the risk of their own lives. When King Nebuchadnezzar commanded them to bow down to the golden image, they stood up to the most powerful man in the world and said, "No! We don't place our faith in a king or a person, we place our faith in the God who will deliver us" (see Dan. 3). God did, in fact, deliver them.

Men and women of valor are like Martin Luther, the great reformer, who defied the kings and priests, tacking his ninety-five theses to the door of the Wittenberg church. He is the man who declared, "In the heat of battle, there the loyalty of the soldier is proved."

Men and women of valor act in utter defiance toward anything that stands between them and the promise God has placed deeply within their spirits. Their victory is forged in the crucible of the conflict that was originally designed to cause their ultimate demise.

And so these sons of Perez, strengthened by the grace of God, must force their way through a narrow opening and endure hardness as good soldiers of Jesus Christ.

VALOR LOOKS DEATH IN THE FACE AND SAYS, "LIVE!"

Smith Wigglesworth was a mighty man of valor. He was a big, two-fisted plumber who wouldn't read any publication but the Bible. Talk about a sanctified life, he wouldn't allow a newspaper to cross the threshold of his home. Every day consisted of reading the Bible for 30 minutes, praying for 30 minutes, reading the Bible for 30 minutes, and praying for 30 minutes until lunch. After a 30-minute break to eat, he repeated the same routine until 6:00 in the evening. He did this seven days a week, except for days when he was preaching.

Many times Dr. Sumrall, my spiritual father, shared stories of Smith Wigglesworth raising people from the dead through the power of God. One story in particular was that in the days before bodies were embalmed, a friend of Smith Wigglesworth died and was laid in a casket. Three days later Wigglesworth visited his departed friend. Believing that it wasn't his friend's time to go, he grabbed the body out of the casket, shoved it up against a wall and shouted, "Live!"

He let go and the corpse fell to the floor with a thud. Again, he picked up the body, shoved it against the wall and shouted, "I told you once, and I'll tell you again. Live!" The body fell to the floor, again. A third time he picked up the body and said, "In the name of the Father, and in the name of the Son, and by the power of the Holy Ghost, I told you three times. I'm not telling you again. Now live!" Then the man coughed and his eyes popped open.

VALOR CALLS FIRE FROM HEAVEN TO JUDGE SIN

Smith Wigglesworth passed his mantle of anointing to Dr. Sumrall. Once, while he was a missionary, a bank raised the interest rates on a loan that he had with them. "I can't afford the payments on the interest rates you're charging me," he told the bank officers. "Is there any way you would reconsider?" When they refused, he told them, "You're thieves and robbers. You either fix it or I'm going to curse you." But they only laughed at him.

Dr. Sumrall left the banker's office, walked into the middle of the street, stretched his arms toward the headquarters of the bank and cursed it. The China Bank at that time was the second largest financial institution in the Orient. Thirty days later, every subsidiary or business associated with the China Bank was insolvent. The doors closed and the building shut down.

Before Dr. Sumrall left this world, he put a sword in my hand, laid his hands on me, and said, "I pray that the faith that is resident in me will come in this young man." Valor isn't confidence in your abilities, it's confidence in God's supernatural ability. Valor isn't faith in your faith, it's faith in God.

DO YOU WANT TO BE COUNTED AMONG THE RANKS OF THE MIGHTY MEN AND WOMEN OF VALOR?

Have you seized the walled cities? Have you stared down the giants in your life? Do you stand in utter defiance to the idolatry of this fallen world? Our great Leader and Liberator, the Lord Jesus Christ, is sifting through the ranks of the self-indulgent and the self-satisfied.

God is looking for people with the spirit of the breaker— mighty men and women of valor who are third-day Christians. People who have faith in the resurrection power that raised Jesus Christ from the dead on the third day. People endowed with fearless courage who focus not on the problem, but on the problem solver.

Make no mistake about it, God will have His day. Soon the time will come when His people, armed with His authority, will rule over this earth.

My question to you is this: Why not you? Why not here? Why not now? You see, not everybody will be a son or daughter of Perez. Jesus preached to thousands, many of whom claimed to follow Him. But on the day of Pentecost only 120 gathered together in the Upper Room. Not everyone is willing to pay the price to be a breaker. Not everyone is willing to take the risk of stepping out in fearless courage.

When you join the ranks of the breakers, you go where you've never been. You give birth to a miracle you didn't even know you were pregnant with. When you choose the way of valor, God places a new spirit in you that gives you the faith to believe that the gates of hell will *not* prevail against you and that *no* weapon formed against you will prosper. Gates of brass and bars of iron break into pieces because you are a breaker, a Holy Ghost–filled, fire-baptized remnant follower of Jesus Christ.

THIS IS THE TIME TO PUSH THROUGH

We've been pushed back and held down long enough. We've been told we wouldn't overcome one time too many. This isn't the time to be cute or pretty. Now is the time to push aside every person, preacher, or prophet who is in the way of our pursuing the high calling of the breaker. God spoke through the prophet Daniel that "the people that do know their God shall be strong, and do exploits" (Dan. 11:32). Jesus said, "The kingdom of heaven suffereth violence, and the violent take it by force" (Matt. 11:12). The kingdom will not be won by namby-pamby Christians who run the moment they face opposition.

After Jesus was killed on the old rugged cross and His body was placed in the cold, stone grave, our Canaan King waded through the ashes of the bygone millenniums of time. He grabbed the devil by the nape of the neck, cast him off his imperial throne, and placed one foot on his throat. There, standing in the midst of Satan's crumbling empire of death, I can only imagine Jesus raised His hands and said to those seeking Him, "I am the Alpha and the Omega, the first and the last. He that was dead is now alive forevermore, and because I live you shall live also!"

VALOR COMES FROM GOD, THE WORD OF GOD, AND IMPARTATION

Perhaps you read about the heroes of the faith in Scripture or you know people who are valiant in the scriptural sense of the word and you say to yourself, *How can I be a mighty man of valor?* or *How can I be a mighty woman of valor?* The faith that breeds fearless courage comes three ways:

First, *faith comes from God.* When you give your life to Jesus Christ, you are infused with a measure of faith. It may lie dormant within you, but you have faith because God has dealt to every Christian a measure of faith (Rom. 12:3). Hebrews 12:2 tells us that Jesus is the author and finisher of our faith. Faith comes from Him (He's the author) and He is the One who brings the object of our faith to its intended goal (He's the finisher). That's why when we align our faith with God's will, miracles happen. Jesus births it, we believe it, and Jesus finishes it. Christians can't say, "I don't have any faith," because if they didn't have faith, they wouldn't be saved.

Second, *faith comes from hearing the Word of God.* Dr. Sumrall once told me, "You don't need more faith, you need to know what faith is." Through God's Word we understand who we are, who God is, and what faith does. Romans 10:17 says, "Faith cometh by hearing, and hearing by the word of God." Our faith flourishes simply by feeding the Word of God into our spirits.

The Bible tells us that the word of God is quick and powerful (see Heb. 4:12). The Greek word for "quick" means "alive."[2] The writer doesn't use the normal word for "life," *bios,* which means a life span with a definite beginning and end. Instead, he uses the word *zoe,* which means "a life that never ends"—the God kind of life that raised Jesus from the grave on the third day. The kind of life we receive when we become Christians. When we consume the living

Word of God into our spirits, it causes a chemical reaction that bolsters our faith.

Third, *faith comes from impartation.* Paul wrote to Timothy,

> When I call to remembrance the unfeigned faith that is in thee, which dwelt first in thy grandmother Lois, and thy mother Eunice; and I am persuaded that in thee also. (2 Tim. 1:5)

Lois was obviously a woman of faith who had the foresight and anointing to nurture and pass on that same faith to her daughter Eunice. Eunice then passed on that anointing to her son Timothy.

Long ago, two men of God, Howard Carter and Smith Wigglesworth, earned their stripes in God's army fighting the good fight of faith. These men of vision had the foresight and anointing to nurture and pass on that faith to another man of God, Dr. Lester Sumrall. He in turn passed on that faith to me.

If you want to do the works of someone you admire, then submit yourself to that person. Serve that person. Seek to know the God of that person.

The principle of impartation is unmistakable in Scripture. Before Elisha was a mighty man of God, he served Elijah. Abraham passed on his faith to Isaac, who passed on his faith to Jacob, who passed on his faith to Judah, who passed on his faith to Perez. Breakers beget breakers and valor begets valor.

When we add impartation and the Word of God to the faith that we already have, great things can't help but happen!

I IMPART MY FAITH NOW TO YOU

I'm not ashamed to tell people that I have faith. People tell me, "You shouldn't say things like that." But I'll declare it from the housetop because I'm possessed by a spirit of faith, and in the name of Jesus

I impart that faith to you through this book. If you have an open heart and a receptive spirit, I believe that you can receive a staggering impartation of the gift of faith.

Now begin calling those things that are not as though they were. Call your baby well. Call your marriage healed. Call your finances blessed. Call that building built. Call that job into being. You are now a mighty man or woman of valor!

CHAPTER 8

PURSUE, OVERTAKE, AND RECOVER ALL

Plumes of smoke billowed up from what he had once called home. Scattered fires were still slowly consuming the little that had been left by the raiding band of nomadic thieves. A lifetime's worth of possessions were stolen, and wives and children were carried away where they would be violated and spend the rest of their lives as slaves.

His troops who had ardently followed him on a variety of dangerous missions and into their last disappointing excursion were now distraught. They had left for only a few days, but upon their return everything was gone. Falling to their knees, the men let out a gut-wrenching cry from a grief they had never before experienced. They threw dirt into the air and onto their heads as each man tried to determine where he would go from here.

The individual cries soon assimilated into a collective anger vented toward the man who had led them away from their families. David, Israel's promised king, faced the real possibility of losing not only his family, but also his life.

Removing himself from his grumbling troops, David sought

the Lord. There, in the presence of God, David's strength was rejuvenated and his confidence restored.

Returning to his men, David asked Abiathar, his priest, to bring the ephod—a vest worn by the priest that also held the Urim and the Thummim. By this time, the disgruntled but curious men were surrounding David and Abiathar because how God would answer through the two precious stones (the Urim and Thummim) would determine what hope they had of getting back what had been stolen.

Abiathar placed the stones in his hands and David asked, "Should we pursue the raiding party? Will we get back what was stolen from us—our wives, our children, and our possessions?" David looked down at his hands to determine what the stones revealed. The men huddled closer. Then God announced,

> Pursue: for thou shalt surely overtake them, and without fail recover all. (1 Sam. 30:8)

The men let out a yell, organized themselves, and with a newfound sense of fearless courage they pursued their enemy. They overtook their enemy. And they recovered everything that had been stolen!

GOD HAS ANOINTED YOU TO PURSUE, OVERTAKE, AND RECOVER ALL

In many ways we're like David: He was anointed, and we are anointed. He was a man of valor; we are a people of valor. His best years were ahead of him; our best years are ahead of us. He was plundered by the enemy; we have been plundered by the enemy.

"Plundered?!?" you may say. Any time you have experienced a financial loss, a premature death of a loved one, a debilitating illness, or a nagging sense of failure, you have been plundered. Many people live their entire lives content with defeat, thinking, *This must be God's will for my life.*

Some Christians haven't even made up their minds whether or not God wants a miracle for them. Some Christians are still arguing, trying to find some way or another to prove that it's not God's will to prosper them. Some are in love with poverty and sickness. They wouldn't want God to heal them because then they wouldn't have anything to talk about.

But Jesus said, "The thief"—that's the devil—"cometh not, but for to steal, and to kill, and to destroy" (John 10:10). The devil's mission in the remaining time before his judgment is to steal, kill, and destroy. He's not out to be nice, he's not out to make friends with you, he's not out on a mercy mission, he's not out to help you get what you want. Satan's sole purpose is to steal, kill, and destroy. Every time you sense him messing with you, know that there are only three things on his mind: stealing, killing, and destroying.

God told David, "You've had enough." There comes a time when enough is enough, when the standoff has to come to an end. There comes a time when negotiation and holding your ground are no longer an option. You may have been raped, pillaged, humiliated, and left for dead, but God has anointed you with the spirit of the breaker to pursue, overtake, and recover everything–everything!–the devil has stolen. The Bible tells us that when the thief is found, he must restore sevenfold everything that he has taken (see Prov. 6:30–31).

THE PROOF OF THE DESIRE IS IN THE PURSUIT

Some people say, "I want my stuff back." But they don't, really. Some people say, "I wish I could be well." But they don't, really. Some people say, "I wish I had more joy" or "I wish I could pay my bills," or "I wish

I could get rid of this pain in my neck." But they don't want it, not really. If you want any of these things, you're going to have to pursue, overtake, and recover all. You can have it all back if you really want it.

An evangelist was once ministering in my church when I said to him, "I wish I could play the piano like you."

"No you don't," he answered back.

"Now wait a minute," I told him. "I'm going to tell you again. I wish I could play the piano like you."

"No, you don't," he answered again.

At this point I was becoming frustrated with his responses, so I asked him, "What are you talking about, saying, 'No, you don't?'"

And then he asked me, "Are you taking any piano lessons?" What could I say? He was right. I didn't *really* want to be as good at the piano as him. He then proceeded to tell me, "The proof of desire is in the pursuit."

You don't really want to be well or have all your needs met or see your children saved or walk in revelation knowledge, or win the victory over the devil unless you're willing to pursue him and take back what was stolen. *The proof of desire is in the pursuit.*

WHO OR WHAT YOU PURSUE
REVEALS YOUR PRIORITIES

I can tell you what you want by what you're chasing. Long ago I chased a beautiful, little Yugoslavian maiden named Joni. For seven years I chased her, and I finally caught her. At that time she lived sixteen miles away, but the road between her home in Kirkersville, Ohio, and my home in Pickerington, Ohio, stayed hot! I wanted to marry that woman, so I pursued her.

Have you ever experienced times when you wonder to yourself, *I can't feel God. I can't see God. I wonder if there is a God?* Do you know where He is? He just stepped back a little bit. All God did was withdraw Himself a little bit to see if you loved Him enough to pursue Him. You have to pursue God if you really want Him.

If you want to recover everything the devil has stolen from you, you're going to have to pursue him, and then you're going to have to overtake him. Most Christians are afraid to take on the principalities and powers of this dark world because of fear. But men and women infused with the spirit of the breaker march forward with fearless courage because they know that they're covered.

HE HAS YOU COVERED

I don't have to tell you that we are in a battle. Look around you and you'll see that skirmishes are being fought all around us. It's good versus evil in a winner-take-all battle. Some Christians are hunkered in a bunker, fearful of the crossfire flying over their heads. Other Christians are prisoners of war, trapped in bondage to sin without any idea how to escape. Still other Christians are safely harbored in the confines of church fortresses far from enemy gunfire. But the remnant army of Jesus Christ is advancing through demonic blockades and barricades designed to slow their pursuit.

There *is* one other detachment of Christians involved in this universal struggle: Men and women are hiding in a foxhole enjoying God's presence. They've been earning their stripes in prayer and worship, and God is about to cut them loose and show them His power. If you're one of those people, this is God's word to you: *Fear not; He has you covered.*

God is about to take you out of your foxhole because He wants you to pursue, overtake, and take back everything your adversary, the devil, has stolen from you. You are shielded and protected, and there is nothing that can get through.

When you're sitting in a foxhole and you're ready to take more ground, you say to your buddy sitting next to you, "Cover me; I'm going in." As you're about to jump out of that holy foxhole, I have good news for you: God's got you covered. You don't have someone with questionable aim backing you up, you have the One who shoots with divine accuracy. Satan is no match for the God who covers us!

Even today, many orthodox and conservative Jewish men wear a skullcap called a *yarmulke* (pronounced ya-ma-ka). The yarmulke is a continual reminder of God's constant presence. Some wear it only when they are at the synagogue, but the more devout Jewish men wear it from the moment they wake up until the moment they go to bed. God is their *yarmulke*, their covering. God is also our yarmulke and we can pursue, overtake, and recover all because He covers us. He is *Jehovah Tsidkenu*, our righteousness; *Jehovah Makaddesh*, our holiness; *Jehovah Shalom*, our peace; *Jehovah Rohi*, our shepherd; *Jehovah Rapha*, the Lord God who heals us.

The God who covers us is also *Jehovah Nissi*, the God who is our banner. The banner was the gathering point in times of war. In order to mobilize the troops, the trumpet would sound and the men would rush to the banner. Then, as the army marched forward, the banner led the way. Even in the heat of battle, the banner remained at the front of the battle line. As long as the banner was in front, the men marched ahead; but when the banner was in retreat, the men would retreat as well.

The banner symbolized the God who covered them.

GOD IS A FAITH GOD

Because we know who is our banner, who has us covered, we can pursue the enemy with fearless courage. The faith of the breaker isn't manufactured or man-made or worked up. The faith that moves mountains and calms the troubled seas is hidden in God. Jesus said in Mark 11:22, "Have faith in God."

God is a faith God, which is why Hebrews 11:6 tells us that without faith it is impossible to please Him. Faith is the intangible implement that enables the breaker to succeed when everyone else fails. Faith in God, our infallible Leader, infuses us with irresistible power that's based on absolute truth.

You don't have to wander in the wilderness wondering, *Is it God's will for me to have joy?* or *Is it God's will to heal me?* or *Is it God's will to prosper me?* It is your Father's good pleasure to give you His kingdom. (Luke 12:32).

- The Bible says, "For the kingdom of God is not meat and drink; but righteousness, and peace, and joy in the Holy Ghost" (Rom. 14:17).

- Jesus commanded His disciples to heal the sick and to tell them, "The kingdom of God is come nigh unto you" (Luke 10:9). Our mandate as disciples of Jesus Christ is to further the kingdom of God on this earth.

- Psalm 35:27 tells us that God takes pleasure in the prosperity of His servant.

You don't have to wander in the wilderness wondering what God's will is for you because He has explicitly revealed it to us in His Word.

The Bible tells us that the way of the wicked is darkness and stumbling (Prov. 4:19). But the way of the righteous is light and clear direction, which comes from God's Word. "Thy word is a lamp unto my feet, and a light unto my path" (Ps. 119:105). Your destiny is not wandering or confusion. Your destiny is believing and knowing through God's Word.

YOU HAVE A RIGHT AND A RESPONSIBILITY TO DRIVE OUT THE ENEMY

Let's look at where the valor of the breaker comes from:

> He that *dwelleth* in the secret place of the most High shall abide under the shadow of the Almighty. (Ps. 91:1, italics added)

> And it shall be, when thou art come in unto the land which the LORD thy God giveth thee for an inheritance, and possessest it, and *dwellest* therein . . . (Deut. 26:1, italics added)

Notice, first of all, that the place where the righteous dwell is secret. Not everyone can find it. Not everyone is willing to pay the price to find it, but God shares it freely with those who pursue an intimate relationship with Him.

Also notice that both passages above share a common Hebrew word that is translated *dwelleth* or *dwellest*. In the same way that we dwell in the secret place is the way that we dwell in the inherited land of promise *after we have possessed it.*

If sickness has taken up residence inside your body or if poverty has taken up residence in your checking account, you have the God-given *right* to drive them out. In fact, you have the God-given *responsibility* to drive them out so you can possess the land.

The Hebrew word for "possess," *yarash,* means "to inherit." In other words, it means to receive what rightfully belongs to you. But it is also a war term that means to drive out the previous tenant. By possessing the land, you are taking back what rightfully and legally belongs to you.

When you possess the land, when you go into battle, everyone knows that the winner gets to keep the spoils. Once you're in the heat of battle, there is no such thing as negotiation, except for an unconditional surrender. War is winner-take-all. To the victor go the spoils.

THE DEVIL SHOOTS SCUDS, BUT WE HAVE PATRIOT MISSILES

The devil is a liar whose bark is much worse than his bite because his weapons are no match for yours. The Bible describes him in 1 Peter 5:8 as a roaring lion . . . he makes a lot of noise and he tells you he's going to hit you with something that isn't even in his possession.

During the Persian Gulf War, the Iraqi army's main weapon was the Scud. These missiles weren't very accurate and they were only effective at short range. But the allied troops had at their disposal Patriot missiles, which could be launched from warships in the Persian Gulf to destroy the incoming missile before it reached its destination.

When Saddam Hussein directed his armies to start shooting their Scud missiles, the opposing armies didn't run in terror. They knew what was coming—it was only a Scud. As the missile approached, they would yell, "Incoming!" but they would also yell, "Outgoing!" because they would send a Patriot missile to blow up the Scud while it was still in the air. On the world's stage, it quickly became apparent that the Iraqis were overmatched.

The moment the devil sits on your shoulder and yells at you, "Incoming!" that's the time you need to stand up and shout in response, "Outgoing!"

When the doctor tells you, "Incoming! You have cancer and your prognosis is terminal," instead of wringing your hands in horror, stand up and shout, "Outgoing! By His stripes I am healed!" (1 Peter 2:24). The Word of God in your mouth is like a Patriot missile:

> So shall my word be that goeth forth out of my mouth: it shall not return unto me void, but it shall accomplish that which I

please, and it shall prosper in the thing whereto I sent it. (Isa. 55:11)

Stop trying to dodge one of Satan's Scuds; launch a counteroffensive. Don't retreat; march forward, possess the land, and drive out the enemy. The Word of God can operate as your Patriot missile, but it can also serve as your laser-guided smart bomb. The Word of God will accomplish that which you please. It is time to learn how to utilize the Word of God and fight against the principalities and powers because God has commanded us to pursue, to overtake, to recover all.

IN ORDER TO DWELL, DIG A WELL

Let's take another look at Deuteronomy 26:1:

> And it shall be, when thou art come in unto the land which the LORD thy God giveth thee for an inheritance, and possessest it, and dwellest therein.

How do you dwell? Often, when a new family or country took possession of the land, they would stake their claim in the area by digging a well (see Gen. 26:25). Wells were essential for life—without water a person could die of thirst within three days. Battles were fought over the possession of wells because lives depended on them. Wells represented life.

Not long ago my daddy, who is in charge of our church building and grounds, sent word to me that they were going to shut off the water. "Why do you have to turn off the water?" I asked him. "We have to shock the well," he replied. "If you're not careful, bacteria will build up in the well, the water will become stagnant, and anyone who drinks the water will get sick. Son, we've got to shock the well."

At that instant, the Holy Ghost jumped inside me and I said to myself, *This is prophetic.* Then God spoke to me, "I'm about to shock the well." In Bible times people would purify a well by pouring salt into it. Today, we shock a well by pouring bleach into it.

God told me, "There are believers who need their wells shocked with some Holy Ghost bleach. They think they have good water, but after I shock their wells, a new power is going to rise up. Fearless courage will well up inside them and they'll become mighty men or women of valor."

If your prayer life is stagnant and you don't have any joy, pray that God will shock you. Jesus said, "He that believeth on me, as the scripture hath said, out of his belly shall flow rivers of living water" (John 7:38). When the living water is flowing out of your spirit, nothing will make you afraid. Nothing will stand in the way of your mandate to pursue, overtake, and recover all.

YOU DON'T HAVE TO BE AFRAID WHEN YOUR DADDY IS BACKING YOU UP

Growing up, our family enjoyed going out for pizza. And we did it a lot. There was one place we would go—Johnny's Pizza—that had just about the best pizza in the world. They made the crust real thin, put that birdseed stuff on the bottom of it, and loaded it up with the little pepperonis that curl up when you bake it.

When I was a little boy about waist-high, we stopped there for some pizza. After we placed our order, my family sat down at a table while I walked over to an area where men were playing shuffleboard. One of the men playing was a pretty rough-looking guy—he wore one of those little black leather hats and chains were dangling down from his black leather vest. Tattoos were all over his arms, and his muscles were bulging everywhere. His motorcycle was parked outside Johnny's Pizza.

The man was playing shuffleboard and I was just watching when something got into me. Right after he slid his disk across the floor, I stuck my foot out, stopped the disk, and slid it back to him. He glared at me and pushed the disk across the floor again. I stuck my foot out, stopped it, and slid it back to him. I was just having fun . . . but he wasn't. He started walking toward me when all of a sudden I felt a leg slide in front of me and a hand grab my shoulder.

"You got something to say to my boy?" The voice behind me was my daddy's. He repeated, "Excuse me, but do you have something to say to the boy? Because you're gonna have to talk to me first." My daddy had me covered.

When the devil comes after you, God says, "I've got you covered." You don't have to be afraid of pursuing, overtaking, and recovering all because He is right behind you, backing you up, and He's walking before you, standing between you and the enemy.

That's why men and women with the spirit of the breaker don't have to be afraid of any Goliath they face, no matter how ominous the person or problem is. They know that God has them covered and that He will empower them to recover everything that has been stolen.

CHAPTER 9

SAFETY IN THE SECRET PLACE

Some of us are sick and tired of being sick and tired. We choose not to run from the adversary, but we choose to pursue him because the fate of the son or daughter of Perez isn't defeat, it's victory. "Pursue . . . overtake . . . recover all" (1 Sam. 30:8). We shouldn't stand idly by and "wait" on the devil to attack us through any means before we take a stand against him. James 4:7 says, "Submit yourselves therefore to God. Resist the devil, and he will flee from you." Resist means to withstand or oppose. But there is a cost. Theodore Roosevelt once said,

> Far better it is to dare mighty things, to win glorious triumphs,
> even though checkered by failure, than to rank with those poor
> spirits who neither enjoy much nor suffer much, because they live
> in the gray twilight that knows not victory nor defeat.

You can't win a battle unless you enter it. But like David, once you know what it's like to climb up on the defeated carcass of your adversary, you're not ready to run back home. You're ready to find another devil to defeat, because victory is contagious.

Victory is also addicting. You win 1 soul, you'll want 10. You win 10, you'll want 100. You win 100, you'll want 1,000. You win 1,000, you'll be like me—chasing a million. I want a million souls!

But your first significant victory is always the hardest. You have to make up your mind beforehand that the devil has defeated you for the last time:

- Your kid's been on crack long enough.

- You are through arguing with your spouse.

- You are done putting up with an unsaved loved one.

- Cancer has claimed its last victim.

- Poverty is no longer a word in your vocabulary.

Now is the time to jump out of the foxhole and win the war!

A DIVINE SETUP

Breaking through the strongholds and barricades that hinder your life doesn't just happen by doing what you've always done. The definition of insanity is repeating the same behavior but expecting a different outcome. You can't get a breakthrough unless you break *through* something. Victory doesn't just happen; it doesn't come to you, you have to pursue it, you have to overtake it. Victory comes only to active contenders, not to idle bystanders.

When the children of Israel were at the Red Sea, they needed a breakthrough miracle. God instructed the children of Israel to set up camp against the Red Sea, and then He hardened Pharaoh's heart so that Pharaoh would send his troops to bring them back.

Why would God send the Israelites into the desert, pin them against the Red Sea, and then send the Egyptians to pursue them?

Because it was a divine setup. God orchestrated the event so the world would see the exceeding greatness of His power.

When you are cornered by sickness, disease, or difficult circumstances, don't pray, *God, why are You letting this happen to me?* God didn't let it *happen* to you. He *orchestrated* the situation so the world would see the exceeding greatness of His power. You see, your "problems" are nothing more than a divine setup. You may see defeat at the end of your situation, but God sees you standing with one foot on Goliath's dead, defeated body.

The Israelites were running from the Egyptians, so God brought them to the Red Sea so they would rely fully on His power to defeat the enemy. Sometimes God rescues us from our pursuers, while other times He expects us to turn around and fight, using the full armor of God:

- The belt of truth.
- The breastplate of righteousness.
- Our feet are shod with the preparation of the gospel of peace.
- The shield of faith.
- The helmet of salvation.
- The sword of the Spirit, which is the Word of God.

. . . but we weren't given anything to protect our backside (see Eph. 6:13–17). As long as we're moving forward, marching toward our enemy, we're safe. But when we turn around and run, that's when we are most vulnerable.

The Israelites needed a breakthrough miracle because they were living out of fear instead of faith. They were reacting instead of acting. So God said, "I'm going to show them how great I really am." The waters parted, and the people walked across the floor of the Red

Sea on dry land. In the end, the Israelites became front-row spectators to a divine confrontation between good and evil.

YOU HAVE THE RIGHT TO CALL FOR BACKUP

In the last chapter, we looked at Psalm 91:1. Let's look at it again:

> He that dwelleth in the secret place of the most High shall abide under the shadow of the Almighty. I will say of the LORD, He is my refuge and my fortress: my God; in him will I trust. (Ps. 91:1–2)

How is God described in this passage?

- The most High
- The Almighty
- My refuge
- My fortress
- The One in whom we place our trust

You see, it's all about God. Our protection from the evil one has nothing to do with us and everything to do with God.

The phrase "I will say of the Lord" can also be translated "I will *declare* of the Lord" or "I will *command* of the Lord."[1] When you are in a difficult situation and you speak out, "I will *say* of the Lord, He is my refuge and my fortress," you are announcing a call to arms and you are acknowledging God's hedge of protection around you.

Your right to call upon the powers of heaven to back you up comes from your inheritance. In Psalm 2:7, God speaks through the psalmist, "I will declare the decree: the LORD hath said unto me, Thou art my Son; this day have I begotten thee." Prophetically, this verse speaks of Jesus, the only begotten Son of God. He was not only the Son of man because He came out of the womb of a woman, He was the Son of God because He was conceived of the Holy Ghost. But prophetically, this verse is also referring to you.

Jesus is the firstborn of the Father and the Lion of the tribe of Judah because He was born in the lineage of David. He is the first-born of the living, but Scripture also tells us that He is the firstborn, or first begotten of the dead (Rev. 1:5). Because you were born in sin, you were counted among the dead. But when you gave your life to Christ, God breathed into you the breath of life and made you a joint heir with Christ (Rom. 8:17).

Jesus was the firstborn of the Father, but because He is in you and you are in Him, you are also considered a firstborn child of God. The firstborn child always gets the birthright, the blessing, the inheritance.

When you're between a rock and a hard place, you can declare, "Lord, *You* are my refuge, *You* are my fortress, *You* are my God in whom I trust," and the angels of heaven will surround you and protect you. They have to because you are a firstborn son, just like Jesus.

You see, God's got you covered! Unfortunately, most Christians are ducking and dodging bullets because they don't realize that they can have backup support if they simply call for it. Others are hiding in a foxhole, terrorized by their adversary.

THE SECRET OF THE SECRET PLACE

There is a secret place for those who place their trust, or their faith, in God. Your faith in God is the key that opens the door to that secret place. But until you learn how to abide in faith, you're exposed.

The nature of a secret is that not everyone knows it. Only certain people are privy to it.

> Thus saith the LORD to his anointed . . . I will go before thee, and make the crooked places straight: I will break in pieces the gates

of brass, and cut in sunder the bars of iron: And I will give thee the treasures of darkness, and hidden riches of *secret* places, that thou mayest know that I, the LORD, which call thee by thy name, am the God of Israel. (Isa. 45:1–3, italics added)

For the froward is abomination to the LORD: but his *secret* is with the righteous. (Prov. 3:32, italics added)

Surely the Lord GOD will do nothing but he revealeth his *secret* unto his servants the prophets. (Amos 3:7, italics added)

God's got a secret, but there aren't many folks who are listening. The secret of the secret place is this: There is a place you can get to in God where the evil one touches you not. But we access that door through faith.

Faith in God can move your mighty mountain. It can cool the fevered brow of your infant child. Faith in God can put money in your bank account that you didn't even deposit. It can make the crooked way straight and the low place high. Through faith in God you can take refuge in the secret place and witness your adversary fleeing before you in seven different directions.

Mighty men and women of valor understand that in order for Satan to get to you, he has to ask for permission. When you're hidden in the secret place, he can't touch you unless God says he can. You're so far inside of God that if the devil grabs for you, all he comes up with is a handful of God.

THERE'S A REQUISITION
WITH YOUR NAME ON IT!

One night Jesus was reclining with His disciples. A dispute broke out between some of them concerning who would be the greatest in the coming kingdom, and Simon Peter was at the center of the debate. Looking across the table, Jesus said, "Simon, Simon, behold, Satan hath desired to have you, that he may sift you as wheat" (Luke 22:31).

Notice the use of double annunciation again? Jesus was saying, "Listen up, Simon. I have something important to say!" And what was it that was so important? Satan desired to sift Simon like wheat; he wanted to test Simon Peter so that his faith would fail. The Greek word for "desire," *exaiteo*, is a cross between "beg" and "demand." You could even translate it as "requisition." Satan earnestly wants you and has filled out a requisition form with your name on it. But Satan couldn't just steal Simon Peter away from God, he had to ask permission!

In the oldest book in the Bible, Job, Satan presented himself before God. God commented to His archenemy how proud He was of Job, but Satan questioned Job's intentions.

> Then Satan answered the LORD, and said, Doth Job fear God for nought? Hast not thou made an hedge about him, and about his house, and about all that he hath on every side? thou hast blessed the work of his hands, and his substance is increased in the land. (Job 1:9–10)

Notice that God placed a hedge around Job that Satan could not penetrate. The only way Satan could touch Job was by God's permission.

> And the LORD said unto Satan, Behold, all that he hath is in thy power; only upon himself put not forth thine hand. So Satan went forth from the presence of the LORD. (Job 1:12)

Before the Resurrection, before Calvary, even before Abraham, Satan had to ask permission from God in order to come against Job. Don't think that God is just sitting by, letting the devil beat your brains out any old time he feels like it. And don't think that when the devil comes after you, you have to run like a dog with your tail tucked between your legs. And most of all, don't think that you have to do something to convince God to help you out of your mess.

Satan has to go through God in order to come near you. But I'm going to let you in on a secret: Satan has already filled out a requisition to come against you and God has already said, "Help yourself."

YOU CAN SURVIVE THE DEVIL'S HIT LIST

The devil has a hit list with the name of every Christian on it. As he works his way down the list, he presents a name before God and asks, "Can I have him?"

"Go ahead and take him if you can handle him," God answers. "If you think you're a match for him, then take him on. But you're going to find more of Me than you find of him."

You're not supposed to be running from the devil the moment hardship manifests itself in your life. "There hath no temptation taken you but such as is common to man: but God is faithful, who will not suffer you to be tempted above that ye are able; but will with the temptation also make a way to escape, that ye may be able to bear it" (1 Cor. 10:13). God will not allow you to face anything greater than what you can handle because His grace is sufficient (see 2 Cor. 12:9). You can weather any storm because greater is He that is in you than he that is in the world (see 1 John 4:4).

Satan requisitioned Peter's life but he wasn't successful, and here's why:

> Simon, Simon, behold, Satan hath desired to have you, that he may sift you as wheat: *But I have prayed for thee, that thy faith fail not.* (Luke 22:31–32, italics added)

The reason Peter didn't fall away from the faith after denying Jesus three times is because Jesus prayed for Peter. It had nothing to do with Peter and everything to do with Jesus! But it wasn't just a general prayer; Jesus prayed that Peter's faith wouldn't fail.

HOW CAN JESUS' PRAYER NOT BE ANSWERED?

After Lazarus was dead and buried in the tomb for four days, Jesus finally arrived in Bethany. Everyone was grief-stricken, and Mary was upset because Jesus hadn't arrived earlier when there might have been a chance for Him to raise Lazarus from the dead. But in a hot climate, bodies decompose quickly and now everyone held little faith in Jesus' power. If Jesus could salvage this situation, it would be His greatest miracle yet.

With the people of Bethany watching, Jesus approached the stone tomb, similar to the one that would hold Him in a few short weeks, and spoke, "Take ye away the stone." The people cautioned Him that doing so would literally cause a stink, but they followed His commands and then Jesus prayed,

> Father, I thank thee that thou hast heard me. And I knew that thou hearest me always: but because of the people which stand by I said it, that they may believe that thou hast sent me. (John 11:41–42)

Lazarus's death and burial were a divine setup. Jesus stood before the tomb and prayed that the people would *believe*—it's the same Greek word for "faith"—that God sent Him. Jesus prayed for the people's faith.

Now let me ask you: Did Jesus ever pray a prayer that the Father did not answer? Of course not. And what is Jesus specifically praying for? That your faith would not fail.

YOU ALREADY HAVE THE FAITH TO OVERCOME

Jesus said, "In the world ye shall have tribulation: but be of good cheer; I have overcome the world" (John 16:33). Jesus has overcome the world and He has given us what we need to overcome the world as well: "This is the victory that overcometh the world, even our faith" (1 John 5:4). In the original Greek manuscript, the word for "even" is missing. A more accurate translation would read: "This is the victory that overcometh the world—our faith." Jesus, whose every prayer is answered by the Father is praying that you would have faith, and that faith which is already resident within you is the power to overcome the world.

Every time I come under attack from the adversary, I form a mental picture in my mind of Jesus' nail-scarred hands and pierced side. I see Him descending into the depths of hell, defeating the devil, death, disease, discouragement, and poverty, and then I see Him ascending with the keys to death, hell, and the grave. After that I see Jesus kneeling before the Father saying,

> Father, I know You allowed the adversary to get through, but he's telling Rod that his son will never be healed. Now Father, I pray for Rod Parsley, that his faith will not fail. The devil's telling him the money will never be there. I stand between him and his adversary and I pray that his faith will not fail.

Then, right in the middle of that satanic attack, something gets on the inside of me and I start saying to myself, *I must have faith; Jesus is praying for it. My faith isn't going to fail me.* If it were dependent on me, it would fail, of course. But Jesus is praying that my faith won't fail.

I have only one question for you: How is your faith going to fail when Jesus is praying that it won't? I don't know why you're believing, but I do know this: There is faith in you right now. You are already endowed with the valor of the breaker to pursue, overtake, and recover *everything* the devil is trying to steal from you.

YOU CAN HIDE IN THE
SECRET PLACE CALLED FAITH

Once, while I was preaching at a crusade in Richmond, Virginia, a woman who was five months pregnant began to scream. I've been to some pretty wild church services, but I have never heard a woman scream like that in church. *She must have a big need,* I said to myself. I tried to keep preaching, but she ran up to me, grabbed me, and wouldn't let me go. And she kept screaming.

Inside her womb was a baby girl whom the doctors had just completed an ultrasound on. They told this lady and her husband that the baby had Edward's disease, a condition where the baby's brain is filled with hundreds of tumors and given little hope of living more than a year. At the very least the baby would be severely mentally retarded. They said, "That's the best you can hope for."

But see, there's a secret place called faith where you can take refuge. Here was this precious woman engaged in the fight of her life. I knew better than to give her some Christian cliché I had read in a book somewhere. What I needed was a revelation of what faith is because this woman needed a miracle. This wasn't a headache that two aspirin would cure.

But when I walked up to her, I wasn't worried. When the enemy comes against you, you don't have to work up your faith. Either you believe or you don't, and if you don't, it's because you don't have a revelation that the answer has nothing to do with you. It's all about Jesus and His finished work on the cross—just as I envision Him when I face an attack from the enemy. Jesus is praying for me, so I don't have to worry. He's got me covered.

So, standing before me and the crowd was a woman, five months pregnant, who needed to take refuge in the secret place. When you hide in the secret place called faith, it doesn't matter what the enemy unleashes on you because God has you covered. X rays showing hundreds of tumors in your baby's brain do not matter because God still has you covered. It doesn't matter if the doctor gives you a terminal diagnosis or your spouse walks out on you or you get laid off from your job. You don't have to worry because God's got you covered.

You see, it's not about *your* faith, but it's about the faith that God has placed inside you and that Jesus Himself is praying for. God is not about to let your faith fail because His reputation is hanging on your miracle.

That night I prayed for the woman and when she returned home, she went back to the doctor for another ultrasound. The ultrasound this time lasted a long time. The mother started praying, wondering to herself, *What's wrong?* Finally, the medical personnel sat down with her and her husband and said, "We can't find anything." Today, she has a healthy child. He's got you covered.

DON'T TRY—JUST TRUST

If you're believing for a miracle, how can it not come to pass? If you're believing for deliverance, how can it not become a reality when Jesus is praying for your faith?

You don't have to try; all you have to do is trust. When facing an attack from the enemy, pray, "Lord, You are my refuge. You are my fortress. You are my God in whom I have faith." Then you can leave the worrying up to God. Because it's really only about Him.

PART IV

VIGOR:
THE STRENGTH OF
THE BREAKER

CHAPTER 10

TAPPING INTO THE DIVINE POWER SOURCE

Our nation is facing a power shortage. California has been in the news recently because they lack the power to meet the needs of the people in their state. As a result, they have experienced rolling blackouts. For hours at a time, businesses are forced to operate without electricity because there isn't enough to go around. And because of the power shortage, the price of tapping into the power source is going up.

The church is no different. We face a power shortage and, like a rolling spiritual blackout, we enjoy the benefits of the power at times, but at other times we suffer from a complete power outage. We pray for the sick but they rarely recover. We share the gospel but few get saved. We proclaim a power that is sporadic at best. But most pathetic of all, we have become content with this sorry state of affairs.

Men and women of vigor, however, are different. They don't draw from the same power source as others; they tap into a never-ending supply that energizes them for whatever task is at hand. They know that power is at a premium, but they gladly pay the price.

Jesus embodied the spirit of the breaker. He was the perfect, sinless man and He was afraid of no one, especially the devil. Jesus was a man of virtue and valor. But He was also a man of vigor—He operated in the power of the Holy Ghost—and He didn't suffer from rolling spiritual blackouts. Every person He touched was healed and every life He encountered was forever transformed. Jesus didn't experience down days because He walked in the power of the Holy Ghost.

Vigor is defined as "physical or mental strength, energy, or force."[1] While the rest of the Christian world plugs into AC power (alternate current), men and women of vigor plug into DC power (direct current). They draw their energy from a supernatural source—the Holy Ghost—who never exhausts His divine power supply. Rolling spiritual blackouts are of little concern to the breaker!

JESUS WAS MORE LIKE US THAN WE'D LIKE TO BELIEVE!

We marvel at the miracles Jesus performed in the Gospels, but many people tell themselves, *I could never do that!* Jesus said we would do greater works than He, but we convince ourselves, *That's easy for Jesus to say. He was God.* Jesus *was* God, but He also laid aside the privileges of His divinity when He came to earth:

> Let this mind be in you, which was also in Christ Jesus: Who, being in the form of God, thought it not robbery to be equal with God: But made himself of no reputation, and took upon him the form of a servant, and was made in the likeness of men: And being found in fashion as a man, he humbled himself, and became obedient unto death, even the death of the cross. (Phil. 2:5–8)

The apostle Paul writes here that when Jesus came to earth, He "made himself of no reputation." A more accurate translation would read that Jesus "emptied Himself." Technically speaking, yes, Jesus was God when He came to earth, but He emptied Himself of His omnipotence (His divine power), His omniscience (His divine knowledge), and His omnipresence (His ability to be everywhere at once) while He was here. Jesus limited Himself to the parameters of humanity in order to completely identify with us.

Jesus was the God-man: all God, all man. Not deity humanized or humanity deified; He was the only God-man who ever walked this planet. We aren't God, we will never be God, we have never been God. But He is God and we are God's, meaning we belong to Him.

When Jesus healed blind Bartimaeus in Mark 10, He didn't draw upon His own divine power to give the man sight because He left his divine attributes in the throne room of glory. So who healed blind Bartimaeus? The God in Christ.

JESUS' POWER CAME FROM THE GOD IN CHRIST

Jesus didn't wipe the blindness out of Bartimaeus's eyes. It was the God in Christ: *Jehovah Rapha*, the God that healeth me. Jesus didn't calm the storm when He spoke, "Peace, be still" (Mark 4:39). It was *Jehovah Shalom*, the God of peace. Jesus didn't place the coins in the fish's mouth when Peter needed to pay their taxes (Matt. 17:27). It was *Jehovah Jireh*, the God who supplies all my needs.

God was physically present *in* Christ! That's why the Bible calls Him "Emmanuel, God with us." God was present in Christ reconciling the world unto Himself (see 2 Cor. 5:19). Jesus laid aside the powers of His divinity and allowed the Holy Spirit to work through Him (see Phil. 2:5–11).

A SURPRISING CONCLUSION
TO THE GOD IN CHRIST

Throughout his ministry, Jesus told His disciples that He would eventually leave them:

> Little children, yet a little while I am with you. Ye shall seek me: and as I said unto the Jews, Whither I go, ye cannot come; so now I say to you. (John 13:33)

> In my Father's house are many mansions: if it were not so, I would have told you. I go to prepare a place for you. (John 14:2)

> Nevertheless I tell you the truth; It is expedient for you that I go away: for if I go not away, the Comforter will not come unto you; but if I depart, I will send him unto you. (John 16:7)

But despite His repeated warnings, the disciples assumed their exciting lives would continue as usual. They had walked with Jesus for three and a half years and gave up everything to follow Him: their livelihoods, their families, their futures, their plans, their programs, their bank accounts. It was a party while He was healing people, multiplying loaves and fishes, and walking on the water.

Then suddenly, one of their own fellow disciples betrayed Jesus for thirty pieces of silver. The disciples watched in horror as He was led before Pilate's parapet to be judged. They couldn't believe their eyes when He was beaten like a common dog, whipped, and then hung on a cross between two thieves. To their shock, Jesus suffered, bled, and died. The heavens convulsed, the sky turned black at midday, and their worlds came crashing down. Their hopes were crushed and their dreams were shattered. After Jesus was buried, the disciples did what any self-respecting person would do when he realizes that the same fate could await him. They hid.

How could Jesus' ministry come to such an abrupt end? What happened to His power source? He was just getting started when He was murdered. After only three and a half years of public ministry, there was no way He was able to finish the work He set out to accomplish. Or maybe not . . .

THE FINISHED WORK OF CHRIST GIVES US WHAT WE NEED HERE ON EARTH

Little did the disciples realize that Jesus' work on earth *was* finished when He allowed Himself to be nailed to the cross. As a result of Jesus' death and resurrection, His finished work provided the basis for our healing, our reconciled relationship with the Father, and our victory over Satan.

The atoning blood of Jesus opens the way for our physical healing. Before Jesus came to earth in bodily form, the prophet Isaiah described His ministry this way,

> But he was wounded for our transgressions, he was bruised for our iniquities: the chastisement of our peace was upon him; and with his stripes *we are healed*. (Isa. 53:5, italics added)

Notice that Isaiah describes Jesus' ministry in the present tense: We *are* healed. Eight hundred years later the apostle Peter described Jesus' ministry of healing through Isaiah's prophecy:

> Who his own self bare our sins in his own body on the tree, that we, being dead to sins, should live unto righteousness: by whose stripes *ye were healed*. (1 Peter 2:24, italics added)

This time, however, Peter doesn't describe Jesus' ministry of healing in the present tense; he uses the past tense: Ye *were* healed. Jesus' work of healing is truly finished and the basis for your healing has already been established.

YOU WERE SAVED BEFORE YOU WERE SAVED

Jesus' finished work provides the basis for our physical healing, but it also provides the basis for our spiritual healing. Our heavenly Father worked through Jesus' earthly ministry to reconcile the world unto Himself (see 2 Cor. 5:18–19). This is important to know if you are believing for the salvation of any loved ones, family members, friends, or work associates. In the mind of God, in the heart of His Son, and through the power of the Holy Spirit, that work of reconciliation is *already* accomplished. It is a finished fact.

Don't put people under condemnation in order to get them saved, because condemnation was not a part of Jesus' ministry. "For God sent not his Son into the world to condemn the world; but that the world through him might be saved" (John 3:17).

Love, however, *was* a characteristic of Jesus' ministry. "For God so loved the world, that he gave his only begotten Son, that whosoever believeth in him should not perish, but have everlasting life" (John 3:16). Our job is to love people and let them know God loves them so much that Jesus died upon a rugged, cruel, bloody beam so they could be reconciled unto Him.

But in the mind of God, we were all saved even before we accepted Jesus. The price was paid in full when Jesus died on the cross for our sins. "For Christ died for sins *once for all*, the righteous for the unrighteous, to bring you to God. He was put to death in the body but made alive by the Spirit" (1 Peter 3:18 NIV, italics added). Jesus paid the price of salvation for the righteous and for the unrighteous once for all. If He didn't, then He would have to die on the cross all over again every time a person accepts Christ.

Our job, then, is to introduce people to Jesus, who has already accepted them. They're not *going* to be accepted. They already *are* accepted in the beloved. All they need to do is receive it! And who was reconciling the world to the Father? It was God in Christ!

SATAN IS *ALREADY* DEFEATED

Before Jesus began His ministry here on earth, the war between good and evil appeared to be at a stalemate. But when He refused to give in to Satan's temptation in the wilderness, the tide of the battle began to turn. Jesus' ministry became the battle line between light and darkness. He healed the sick and multiplied the loaves and fishes, but He also cast out demons. Satan repeatedly tried to use the spiritual leaders to assassinate Jesus, but they were unsuccessful. Until the Cross.

Satan thought he had won the war when Jesus was nailed to that lonely tree. But on the third day, Satan's fate was sealed when Jesus rose from the dead. Jesus' resurrection proved once for all that sin, sickness, disease, and death held no power over Him.

The war is over. Until he is thrown into the lake of fire, Satan is dragging down as many people as he can. And, he's trying to neutralize the body of Christ. No one threatens him like a Christian with the spirit of the breaker.

Some Christians wrongly assume that we're still engaged in a war. But the war is over: Satan lost! However, skirmishes continue to be fought. We move forward in the spirit of the breaker by putting on the armor of God, casting out demons, and binding the enemy. But we do so from the perspective that we remind Satan of his defeat. We appropriate the victory of Jesus over Satan into our present situations.

JESUS LEFT HIS DISCIPLES BUT HE
DIDN'T ABANDON THEM

After Jesus' glorious resurrection, the disciples asked Him, "So, when are You going to get around to restoring the kingdom of Israel?" They wanted to show the people—especially the Jewish leaders—who was now on top. Nobody was going to push them around anymore! But they wrongly assumed that Jesus' kingdom was a *physical* kingdom. They didn't realize that the kingdom of God was going to be advanced in human hearts. It was foremost a *spiritual* kingdom.

In their minds they saw themselves as victors returning from battle, with Jesus leading the way. But then Jesus said, "Not so fast. I'm not here to stay, because I'm going back to My Father." They were stunned.

Talk about a roller-coaster ride! First Jesus is alive, then He's dead, then He's alive again, and then He says He's leaving. "What do You mean You're leaving?" they asked Him. Jesus then instructed the disciples to tarry in Jerusalem until the Holy Spirit empowered them with the vigor of the breaker:

> And, being assembled together with them, [Jesus] commanded them that they should not depart from Jerusalem, but wait for the promise of the Father, which, saith he, ye have heard of me. For John truly baptized with water; but ye shall be baptized with the Holy Ghost not many days hence . . . But ye shall receive power, after that the Holy Ghost is come upon you: and ye shall be witnesses unto me both in Jerusalem, and in all Judaea, and in Samaria, and unto the uttermost part of the earth. (Acts 1:4–5, 8)

Jesus was returning to the Father, but He wasn't abandoning the disciples. He wasn't going to leave them comfortless because He was going to send them the Comforter. "It is expedient for you that I go away: for if I go not away, the Comforter will not come unto you; but if I depart, I will send him unto you" (John 16:7). Jesus said it was necessary that He go away, because then the Comforter would come. As long as Jesus was physically present with the disciples, the Holy Ghost would operate only through Jesus. But when Jesus ascended to the Father, then the Holy Ghost would be free to operate through the disciples in the same way that He operated through Jesus.

Here is where many Christians miss it: They believe that the Holy Ghost is some kind of watered-down version of God—a second cousin three times removed from the Father. But the Holy Ghost is as much God as the Father or the Son. They all are one in essence and quality.

Just as the Holy Ghost worked through Jesus, Jesus would send the Holy Ghost to work through His followers. After He instructed the disciples to remain in Jerusalem, He ascended to heaven.

The 120 remnant followers of Jesus Christ tarried in Jerusalem for ten days, seeking the promised Holy Spirit. They didn't know what to expect, but they followed Jesus' commands. Then, on Pentecost Sunday, while they were together in the Upper Room, the Holy Ghost filled the room and more so, the people in the room, giving them the power to be witnesses and to perform the same works as Jesus.

THE GOD IN CHRIST IS NOW THE CHRIST IN YOU

In Matthew, Mark, Luke, and John we read about the God in Christ. But when we read the book of Acts, the God in Christ becomes the Christ in you. When Jesus ascended to heaven, He did a tag-team handoff with the Holy Ghost. Jesus went up and the Holy Ghost came down! We give our lives to Christ, and He gives to us the Holy Ghost.

The Holy Ghost, the same in essence and quality as the Father and Son, now indwells every believer. It's no wonder Jesus said, "He that believeth on me, the works that I do shall he do also; and greater works than these shall he do; because I go unto my Father" (John 14:12). We can tap into the same power supply that Jesus did when He was here on earth.

If Christ is God and the Holy Ghost is God, then God lives inside your body! The same Spirit that raised Jesus from the dead now lives in you (Rom. 8:11), and the Spirit of the Prince of breakers now lives in you!

WE DON'T WANT TO SIN WHEN WE'RE FILLED WITH THE HOLY GHOST

Many Christians proclaim, "I'm filled with the Holy Ghost." But here's how you know if it's really true: They don't want to sin. When you're filled with the Holy Ghost, sin no longer holds a grip on your life. Like Jesus, you have the power to withstand temptation. No longer do you want to lie, cheat, and steal. Pornography and sexual perversion are repulsive to you.

How are you going to be a backbiter or a talebearer and still be full of the Holy Ghost? How are you going to fornicate when the same Spirit that raised Christ from the dead is living in you? When you're full of the Holy Ghost, you have no room for sin. But the less Holy Ghost you have in you, the more room you make for sin.

People who claim to be filled with the Holy Ghost but still wallow in sin aren't fooling anybody. They might have been filled at one time, but they aren't filled now.

THE FRUIT OF THE INFILLING

The Holy Ghost manifests Himself through people who are filled. First, they yield the fruit of the Spirit: love, joy, peace, longsuffering, gentleness, goodness, faith, meekness, and temperance (Gal. 5:22–23). The fruit of the Spirit is simply the fruit of the Spirit's work in a Christian's life. You can't be a mean person and be filled with the Spirit at the same time.

People filled with the Holy Ghost also make spiritual babies. Immediately after being filled with the Spirit, the believers described in Acts chapter 2 shared the gospel with the people in Jerusalem. That day, three thousand men alone, plus women and children, became believers. This fulfilled Jesus' words in Acts 1:8:

> But ye shall receive power, after that the Holy Ghost is come upon you: and ye shall be witnesses unto me both in Jerusalem, and in all Judaea, and in Samaria, and unto the uttermost part of the earth.

The purpose of the power is for people to proclaim the good news of salvation through Jesus Christ. The power of the Holy Ghost is poured out and people are empowered to be witnesses.

If you're not making spiritual babies, I don't care how much you talk in tongues. I don't care how much you prophesy. What you're doing makes no difference. If you are not giving birth to spiritual babies, if you don't have a passion for souls, you do not have the baptism in the Holy Ghost!

THE POWER COMES AT A PRICE

Jesus said, "Blessed are they which do hunger and thirst after righteousness: for they shall be filled" (Matt. 5:6). If you want more of God, you have to hunger for Him. When you're hungry for God, the things of this world lose their luster. Everything else seems trivial. The food on your plate doesn't taste the same. The programs on television lose interest to you. When you hunger and thirst after righteousness, look out! You're about to be filled!

If you aren't hungry, God is not going to fill you with the Holy Ghost because He refuses to give people something they don't want. But if you are unsatisfied with rolling spiritual blackouts, you need to know that plugging into the direct-current power supply of the Holy Ghost comes at a cost.

Tapping into the power of the Holy Ghost will cost you your reputation. Remember that Jesus made Himself of no reputation when He came to earth (Phil. 2:7). He didn't care what people thought of Him. If you're unwilling to share Jesus with your coworkers because you're afraid of what they will think, then don't expect to tap into God's divine power supply.

Pentecost wasn't popular with the Jewish leaders in the early church, and it isn't popular today, either. Not *real* Pentecost. The church today tries to mainstream Pentecost. They want to make it respectable, dignified, and socially acceptable. "Tongues are for the prayer closet but not for public worship," they say. But when the Spirit was poured out in Acts chapter 2, the church spoke in tongues, not just in church, but on the city streets! Their conduct was so undignified that bystanders thought the Christians were drunk.

To the man and woman of vigor, reputation and ridicule mean nothing. Jesus promised,

> Blessed are ye, when men shall revile you, and persecute you, and shall say all manner of evil against you falsely, for my sake. Rejoice, and be exceeding glad: for great is your reward in heaven: for so persecuted they the prophets which were before you. (Matt. 5:11–12)

The price of Pentecostal power is paid with our reputations. The favor of God may cost you the favor of men and banishment from organized religion. To people in the New Testament church, it also meant prison and persecution. We like to shout "hallelujah" knowing that God lives in us, but we don't get as excited knowing what it will cost us. If you want power over deception, power over disease, power over devils, and power over depravity, then you have to be willing to count the cost.

DO YOU WANT THE POWER?

The price of the power is high, but the benefits of the power are divine! Jesus promised that if you pay the price, you will take up serpents and not be harmed. You will drink any deadly thing and not be hurt. You will lay hands on the sick, and the sick will be healed (Mark 16:17–18). You can look sin in the eye and say, "Take a backseat. I'm full of the Holy Ghost."

Don't seek the newfangled thing. Seek the power of Pentecost. Tell yourself, *The God in Christ has become the Christ in me.* Let the Lion of the tribe of Judah roar from the inside of your being until it's not you roaring, but Christ.

You don't have to be content with rolling spiritual blackouts. You can be plugged into the *direct* current of the divine power source when the rest of the church is plugged into the *alternate* current! You can be a man or woman of vigor because the God in Christ has become the Christ in you.

CHAPTER 11

THE PASSING-THROUGH ANOINTING

What would you think if your pastor stood up in church one Sunday, read a prophecy from the book of Isaiah, and then announced that he was the fulfillment of that prophecy? If you have any common sense, you would either leave the church or run that pastor out of town. Anyone making such a ludicrous claim must be either crazy or cultic.

And that's exactly how most people responded to Jesus.

Immediately following His temptation in the wilderness, Jesus began His ministry by going to His hometown synagogue in Nazareth where His family and friends attended church every week. Jesus volunteered to give the Scripture reading for the worship service that morning and walked to the front of the congregation.

As He slowly and carefully unrolled the scroll, the people must have been relieved that Jesus returned safely from His long, mysterious trip into the wilderness. He was such a nice young man and so respectful. The care He showed His mother, Mary, made her the envy of the other widows in the community.

Turning, then, to the book of Isaiah, Jesus read the following words,

> The Spirit of the Lord is upon me, because he hath anointed me to preach the gospel to the poor; he hath sent me to heal the brokenhearted, to preach deliverance to the captives, and recovering of sight to the blind, to set at liberty them that are bruised, to preach the acceptable year of the Lord. (Luke 4:18–19)

As was the custom of that time, Jesus rolled up the scroll, handed it to the synagogue attendant, and then sat down in the very seat reserved for the coming Messiah where He would begin to teach. Silence filled the room as the people waited to hear Jesus' words. Since His return from the wilderness, His teaching ministry had become quite well known, and the people were eager to hear what Jesus had to say. Then He uttered the words that would separate Jesus from many of His family and friends for the duration of His earthly ministry:

> This day is this scripture fulfilled in your ears. (Luke 4:21)

At first the people didn't think they heard correctly. Did Jesus say He was the fulfillment of Isaiah's prophecy? Was Jesus claiming that *He* was the Messiah? He must have spent too much time in the heat while He was in the desert! His words were powerful, but this wasn't the Jesus they knew. Jesus couldn't be the Messiah; why, they had watched Him grow up! Some of the women had even cared for Him as a baby.

Sensing their skepticism, Jesus' gracious words became increasingly direct, and the people grew increasingly agitated. "No prophet is welcome in his hometown," Jesus told them, "and you're no different. If you and the rest of our people don't heed My words, I will take

God's message and ministry to the Gentiles, just as Elijah and Elisha did." The thought of God working among the Gentiles at the exclusion of the Jews was an affront. Who did Jesus think He was? God?

The once-passive crowd soon turned into an angry mob. And the more they thought about Jesus' words, the angrier they became. Past friendships no longer mattered; they were going to deal with Jesus once and for all. Dragging Him out of the synagogue, the crowd began walking toward a nearby cliff where they planned to throw Him onto the rocks below and then stone Him. When they reached the edge of the cliff, they looked around to see who was carrying Jesus. But He was gone. Where did He go?

> But he passing through the midst of them went his way. (Luke 4:30)

Jesus wasn't apprehended because He walked in the passing-through anointing.[1]

THE ANOINTING MAKES YOU A TARGET

The anointing of a breaker is invigorating but also dangerous. People enjoy the fruit of the anointing until that man or woman begins challenging what is near and dear to their hearts. Then the people become like a mama bear robbed of her cubs.

The anointing attracts the favor of God, but it also makes us a target of the enemy. If the anointing breaks the yoke of the enemy, why would the enemy leave us alone? We're the only ones with the ability to bring him down! Therefore, every anointed man or woman lives with an invisible target taped to his or her back.

Fortunately, the anointed man or woman of God is endowed with the vigor of the breaker. "Greater is he that is in you, than he that is in the world" (1 John 4:4).

THE PROOF OF THE ANOINTING
IS IN THE POWER

The opposition may be great, but the power within you is greater. King David wrote, "By this I know that thou favourest me, because mine enemy doth not triumph over me" (Ps. 41:11).

When the favor of God rests upon you, sickness and disease can't handle you. Addictions can't bind you. Financial problems can't rule over you. Chains break asunder.

The favor of God isn't proved by the fancy clothes you wear or the fame you have. The favor of God isn't proved by the nice car you drive or the number of people who attend your Bible study. The favor, the anointing, of God is proved by this: The enemy doesn't triumph over you. The proof of the anointing is in the power. It's the passing-through anointing.

Homosexual spirits run from your presence. Leukemia dies because no enemy can triumph over you. Satan, sickness, and sin bow their knee. Demons, depravity, and disease loose their hold.

> No weapon that is formed against thee shall prosper; and every tongue that shall rise against thee in judgment thou shalt con-demn. This is the heritage of the servants of the LORD, and their righteousness is of me, saith the LORD. (Isa. 54:17)

Victory against our enemies is our heritage: "Now thanks be unto God, which always causeth us to triumph in Christ" (2 Cor. 2:14).

IN THE WORLD, BUT NOT OF THE WORLD

Victory may be the heritage of the church, but few people ever enjoy their inheritance. The problem with most Christians is that many are saved but don't enjoy all of the benefits salvation brings.

They want just enough of Jesus to squeeze through those pearly gates.

In Chapter 4, I shared that Christians are sanctified *from* the world and *to* God. But in the same turn some Christians—who do not have a total revelation of the fullness of salvation—have been delivered *from* the world, but they haven't been delivered *to* God. They may have been delivered from drugs, but they haven't been delivered to a complete and total Holy Ghost indwelling. They may have been delivered from perversion, but they haven't been delivered into joy and dancing.

Sometimes I look into the eyes of someone who has been delivered from addiction, pain, disease, depression, or financial lack and I think, *They were happier with their old lifestyle* because it's obvious that they aren't enjoying all the fringe benefits of the kingdom. Not that I would want people to return to their old lives, but because they haven't spiritually matured, they only operate in the arm of the flesh.

THE ARM OF THE FLESH ALWAYS
GETS YOU IN A MESS

At first, Moses sought to deliver the children of Israel using the arm of the flesh. Knowing he was destined to deliver his fellow Israelites from bondage, he tried to accomplish in the physical what can only be accomplished in the spiritual. When Moses attempted to rescue only one Israelite, he slayed an Egyptian in the process (see Ex. 2). Moses could identify the problem—his people were in bondage—but he had no idea how to deliver them.

Like Moses, some Christians understand the bankruptcy of bondage. They realize that sickness and scarcity aren't a part of God's plan. But because they try to overcome using the arm of the flesh, they fail. Preachers try to use their Las Vegas personality to move those from bondage into freedom, but their efforts are in vain.

Charisma, physical strength, wealth, and intellect mean nothing when dealing in the spiritual realm.

Moses was one of the most educated, charismatic, and wealthiest men in all of Egypt. Growing up in Pharaoh's house, he was raised in the lap of luxury. This man of privilege ate the finest foods and exemplified the model Egyptian. If anyone would be able to deliver Israel based upon ability, it was Moses. But he trusted in the arm of the flesh. And the arm of the flesh will always get you in a mess.

In order to reeducate him, God sent Moses into the desert to attend the school of the Holy Ghost. For forty years, God trained him in the ways of the Spirit. And upon his graduation, Moses encountered Jehovah in a burning bush on the side of Mount Horeb. "I'm sending you back to your people," God told Moses. "But this time, *I* will deliver them" (see Ex. 3:8).

You see, it's not about us, it's about Him. It's not about your strength, it's about His sovereignty. It's not about your goodness, it's about His grace. It's not about your merit, it's about His mercy. God will work through you to deliver people from bondage in His strength and timing, not yours.

Breakers endued with vigor from above are not powerless because they avoid operating from the weak arm of the flesh. On the contrary, they are mighty because they operate in the strong arm of the Lord.

Once Moses learned how to operate in the strong arm of the Lord, three million Israelites were delivered, and a bead of sweat never formed on Moses' brow. Why? Because he had a passing-through anointing.

IF WHAT YOU'RE DOING ISN'T WORKING—STOP IT!

Joshua learned the importance of the passing-through anointing from his mentor, Moses. He was just a young man when Moses led the children of Israel as they passed through the Red Sea on dry land. He carefully observed his mentor when the Amorites refused to allow Israel to pass through their territory on the way to the promised land.

After Moses died, Joshua inherited the passing-through anointing so that when they reached the Jordan River, he knew what to do. He didn't force his way across the surging river, risking the people's lives and livestock.

Knowing the importance of being led by the Spirit of God, Joshua instructed the Levites transporting the ark of the covenant to walk at the front of the mass of people. Then he gave them these orders, "When ye are come to the brink of the water of Jordan, ye shall stand still in Jordan" (Josh. 3:8). He didn't say, "Try to swim across the river." He said, "Once you reach the edge of the Jordan, stand in the river and wait for God to do something." The Levites obeyed Joshua's command, the waters parted, and the people of Israel passed through on dry land. It was the passing-through anointing.

Some Christians are guided by the motto "If it jams, force it. If it breaks, it needed fixing anyway." They try to make things happen because they're too impatient to wait on God. They act first and then pray. They lose money on bad investments because they didn't begin by seeking God's direction. They confront people's sin without waiting on God's timing to do it. And in the process they hurt themselves and often the people around them.

If what you're doing isn't working, then stop doing it. Stop preaching the way you've been preaching. Stop depending on what you've been depending on. Stop praying the way you've been praying because if the answer was in that, you wouldn't be in bondage right now. You would be in freedom. Obviously, the way you're doing it isn't working, so maybe it's time to wait on God and do it His way.

When you sense you are on the brink of your breakthrough, stand still! Let God part the waters before you jump into the river and make a big mistake.

PASSING THE POINT OF NO RETURN

Once the people crossed the Jordan and entered the promised land, they knew they had passed the point of no return. They were backed against the water and faced an enemy they would have to displace. Unless they were led by the Spirit of God, Israel held no hope.

God often backs us against the wall so we will rely on His arm. He takes us past the point of no return to deliver us from our complacent, lackadaisical lives filled with bondage, fear, and discouragement. Superior Bible knowledge won't move you forward; you need the passing-through anointing. And often, where God guides makes no sense whatsoever.

The promised land wasn't anything like Egypt. God warned them,

> For the land, whither thou goest in to possess it, is not as the land of Egypt, from whence ye came out, where thou sowedst thy seed, and wateredst it with thy foot, as a garden of herbs: But the land, whither ye go to possess it, is a land of hills and valleys, and drinketh water of the rain of heaven. (Deut. 11:10–11)

Goshen, where the Israelites lived in Egypt, was situated on a river delta. The soil was fertile and although rain was sparse, the farmers had plenty of water for their fields because their irrigation ditches drew an endless supply of water from the Nile River.

The promised land, however, was a place of hills and valleys, of rock and granite. The Jordan River might overflow in the spring, but it might be completely dry by summer. So, Israel would have to rely primarily on the rain—which could be very sporadic—and ultimately the God of rain, to supply their needs. Relying on the ever-present Nile wasn't a test of faith; relying on God was.

Everything in the new kingdom where God is taking His people is diametrically opposed and mutually exclusive to everything in the kingdom that He delivered us from. The world tells us, "If you want to climb the ladder of success, you must claw your way to the top and step on anyone who stands in your way."

But in God's kingdom, up is not up. Up is down. Jesus said, "And whosoever shall exalt himself shall be abased; and he that shall humble himself shall be exalted" (Matt. 23:12). Henri Nouwen wrote, "The way of the Christian leader is not the way of upward mobility in which the world has invested so much, but the way of downward mobility ending on the cross."[2]

Do you want to receive? Don't grab for the gusto, for in the kingdom of God, to give is to receive. In the old kingdom, if you wanted to live, you had to fight for your rights. But in the new kingdom, if you want to live, Jesus said, you have to die: "Whosoever shall seek to save his life shall lose it; and whosoever shall lose his life shall preserve it" (Luke 17:33).

If you want to live in the vigor of the breaker and walk with the passing-through anointing, then you must refuse to operate in the arm of the flesh. You must be led by the Spirit of God. "For as many as are led by the Spirit of God, they are the sons of God" (Rom. 8:14).

THE MYSTERY OF GOD'S WISDOM IS HIDDEN FOR YOU, NOT FROM YOU

So often we try to figure everything out in our mind, but God says, "Forget what you've learned." The Bible tells us, "But we speak the wisdom of God in a mystery, even the hidden wisdom, which God ordained before the world unto our glory" (1 Cor. 2:7).

You're not going to find God's wisdom thinking what you've always thought. God's wisdom resides in the spirit realm, which cannot be accessed from the physical realm. The arm of the flesh cannot reach it, and the intellectual mind cannot grasp it.

The mystery of God's wisdom, however, isn't hidden *from* you, but *for* you. God hid your answer where the devil cannot find it because if Satan had it, he would be like God. Had Satan known the mysteries of God, he would have figured out a way to neutralize Jesus' passing-through anointing that day in Nazareth.

If you have ever been in a house of mirrors at a carnival or amusement park, then you understand what the devil has to deal with when he encounters people who have the passing-through anointing. You walk through what you think is a doorway, but you collide with a mirror and bloody your nose. You reach out to touch your friend, but you bruise your knuckles.

When the passing-through anointing comes on you, the devil can't touch you because he can't find you. You pass through troubled waters without being troubled. Worry and anxiety can't stick to you because you're clothed with Holy Ghost Teflon. The devil sets a trap and when he returns, the trap is sprung but you're not hung. It's the passing-through anointing.

Men and women endowed with the vigor of the breaker realize that the solution to their problems resides in God's power, not their power. They don't ask God, "What am I going to do?" They ask God, "What are *You* going to do?" They pray, "Here's my sickness, my sin, my poverty, my kids—what are *You* going to do about it?" The answer may be a mystery, but they know where to go to solve it.

WE ACCESS THE MYSTERIES OF GOD BY PRAYING IN THE POWER OF THE HOLY GHOST

Likewise the Spirit also helpeth our infirmities: for we know not what we should pray for as we ought: but the Spirit itself maketh intercession for us with groanings which cannot be uttered. And he that searcheth the hearts knoweth what is the mind of the Spirit, because he maketh intercession for the saints according to the will of God. (Rom. 8:26–27)

When you pray in the Holy Spirit, your spirit prays and your mind is unfruitful. Your mind resides in the natural, but your spirit resides in the supernatural. Anything residing in the natural can be affected by the god of this world, but when you pray in the spirit, you enter that place where Satan cannot touch you. It's the passing-through anointing.

By praying in the power of the Holy Ghost, you're telling that miracle how to show up in your body. You're telling that money to be deposited in your bank account. You're calling your prodigal child home. You're fighting the devil in a realm that renders him utterly defenseless. When you pray in tongues, you are praying along the lines of God's perfect will, releasing a power that is unparalleled by any force the prince of this world can counter. The flesh is neutralized and your spirit is energized.

YOU'RE LIKE A STEALTH BOMBER

During the Persian Gulf War, thousands of allied sorties were flown over enemy-held territory. From our homes halfway across the world we watched live television reports aired from Baghdad, Iraq. In the background we could see antiaircraft guns firing into the air. If you were like me, you probably wondered, *How can our aircraft fly through such a heavy bombardment of artillery?*

A key component in the allies' success was the Stealth Bomber. The plane's rounded curves and high-tech composite materials helped it absorb or deflect enemy radar signals. The strategic placement of the engine and exhaust vents helped hide the aircraft from heat-seeking sensors. Despite the heavy artillery fire, not one Stealth Bomber recorded so much as a scratch on its hull. Now that's what you call a passing-through anointing!

Through the power of the Holy Ghost, we become Stealth Bombers avoiding and evading detection from the enemy's radar screen. When you pray in the Holy Spirit, Satan simply cannot find you.

People might try to throw you off the mountain of your miracle, but you can be like Jesus and pass through the midst of them. You can walk in the passing-through anointing because you have the vigor of the breaker!

In the next chapter we will look more closely at how you can put on the Holy Ghost composite materials that enable you to slip under the enemy's radar screen.

CHAPTER 12

THE CLOTHING MAKES
THE MAN . . . AND WOMAN

Israel was distraught. Midianite raiders were slowly strangling what little life still existed in the people. The desert intruders decimated the people's crops, destroyed their animals, and defeated anyone who stood in their way. With barely any means to support themselves, God's chosen people were dying a slow death. Why would God empower them to possess the promised land only to allow them to perish less than a hundred years later?

The people were powerless at the hands of their enemies, but they were also powerless in their walk with God. Because they replaced their worship of Jehovah with the worship of Baal, God removed His presence from His people. And as a result, the nation experienced the hopelessness and helplessness that come from forsaking the God of Israel.

Just as many people do today when they run out of options to save themselves, Israel cried out to God. He answered their prayer, but He didn't use the bravest man in the kingdom to meet their request.

We first meet this man as he is hiding in a winepress trying to thresh wheat for flour. Threshing floors at that time were located at the top of the highest hill in the area so the wind could blow the chaff away when the thresher threw the grain into the air. Winepresses, on the other hand, were located at the foot of the hill so the workers could carry their grapes downhill from the vineyards. But the man, not wanting to risk his meager crop or his life, chooses to hide from his enemies in order to thresh his grain. So there the next great leader of Israel hides, tossing his wheat into the air, but the chaff isn't blowing away because the hills are shielding him from the wind.

Growing increasingly frustrated with the futility of his labor and the cowardice of his character, Gideon pauses a moment to catch his breath. Looking up, he is startled by a man sitting under an oak tree. "The LORD is with thee, thou mighty man of valour" (Judg. 6:12), the angel of the Lord tells him. Strange words from a strange man. This man, the pre-incarnate Christ, then encourages Gideon, "Go in this thy might, and thou shalt save Israel from the hand of the Midianites: have not I sent thee?" (Judg. 6:14).

During this divine encounter with the angel of the Lord, Gideon is instructed to desecrate a local altar to Baal and build next to it an altar to Jehovah. This "mighty man of valor," however, waits until the dark of night to obey because he is afraid of his own people. The next day the people discover what Gideon has done, but God spares Gideon's life from his angry kinsmen.

God intervenes in Gideon's life, yet Gideon is no different than he was before his encounter with the pre-incarnate Christ at the winepress—until the Midianites, Amalekites, and other Canaanite tribes mobilize forces to utterly destroy the people of Israel. Then something happens to Gideon that forever changes his life.

CLOTHE YOURSELF WITH GOD'S POWER

Then the Spirit of the LORD *came upon* Gideon, and he blew a trumpet, summoning the Abiezrites to follow him. He sent mes-

sengers throughout Manasseh, calling them to arms, and also into
Asher, Zebulun and Naphtali, so that they too went up to meet
them. (Judg. 6:34–35 NIV, italics added)

The words "came upon" mean, literally, "clothed." The Spirit of the
Lord *clothed* Gideon. Like a garment, the Spirit of the Lord clothed
Gideon with the power, the vigor of the breaker, to lead the children
of Israel against their enemies.

The idea of clothing ourselves with the Spirit of God is fairly
common in Scripture. Through the prophet Isaiah, God urged the
inhabitants of Zion to clothe themselves with His strength:

> Awake, awake; put on thy strength, O Zion; put on thy beautiful
> garments, O Jerusalem, the holy city: for henceforth there shall
> no more come into thee the uncircumcised and the unclean. (Isa.
> 52:1)

The apostle Paul urged the church of Ephesus to "put on"—from
the Greek word for "clothe"—themselves the whole armor of God
(Eph. 6:11). But most important, Christians are reminded that they
are clothed with Christ:

> For ye are all the children of God by faith in Christ Jesus.
> For as many of you as have been baptized into Christ have
> *put on* Christ. (Gal. 3:26–27, italics added)

And really, when we clothe ourselves with the armor of God, we are
clothing ourselves with Christ. Jesus is Truth, our righteousness and
our peace. Our faith and salvation rest solely in Him, and He is the
living Word of God (see Eph. 6:14–17).

Men and women endued with the spirit of the breaker are filled
with the Spirit and clothed with Christ.

POSSESSED BY THE SPIRIT OF GOD

Before he was clothed with the spirit of God, Gideon cowered in fear. He was powerless to do exploits. He was just like anyone else. The clothing truly makes the man or woman.

But the Hebrew word for "clothe" doesn't just mean clothe as with a jacket; it also means that the Spirit of God took possession of or was incarnated in Gideon.[1] Gideon became a man possessed by the Spirit of God.

God looked at the threat of Israel's extinction and, since He is Spirit, said, "I want a body to accomplish My purposes." When He chose Gideon, He picked him up and put Gideon on, just like a jacket. God incarnated Himself inside Gideon.

God wants to put you on, too. He wants to wrap you around Himself so that when you move, it's not you moving, but Him. God wants to incarnate Himself inside you. We in turn need to say, "Holy Ghost, wrap me around You. Step into my shoes and walk through me. Wear me like a jacket and move through me. I want to be clothed with the Holy Ghost."

WE ARE FIRST OF ALL SPIRIT BEINGS

In order to walk with the vigor of the breaker, the church must understand that we are first of all spirits who live in a body. Our spirit and body are inseparable while we live here on earth, but nevertheless, we are essentially spirit beings.

God formed man out of the dust of the earth. That's all Adam was—a hunk of dirt. God said, "For dust thou art, and unto dust shalt thou return" (Gen. 3:19). What you see when you look in the mirror is not really you. It's dust. That's why people can't look at you and know the real you.

What made the difference between Adam and a pile of dust? The breath of God. "And the LORD God formed man of the dust of the ground, and breathed into [Adam's] nostrils the breath of life; and man became a living soul" (Gen. 2:7).

PENTECOST IS THE REINCARNATION OF CREATION

Jesus told the church to tarry in Jerusalem until they were "endued with power from on high" (Luke 24:49). The Greek word *enduo*, from which we get the word *endued*, means—you guessed it!— "clothed." Jesus told the disciples to wait until they were clothed with power from on high. Gideon and the New Testament church were power dressers!

On the day of Pentecost, God didn't send a cool summer breeze; He sent a rushing, mighty wind. "And suddenly there came a sound from heaven as of a rushing mighty wind, and it filled all the house where they were sitting" (Acts 2:2).

The word for "Spirit" in the Hebrew Old Testament is *breath* (*ruach*) and the word for "Spirit" in the Greek New Testament is *wind* (*pneuma*). The wind in Acts chapter 2 is the reincarnation of God's breath in Genesis chapter 2. The baptism of the Holy Ghost is a re-creation of our creation.

The reason God gave you a body is to accomplish His will through you. The apostle Paul wrote, "But we have this treasure in earthen vessels, that the excellency of the power may be of God, and not of us" (2 Cor. 4:7). We're just dirt pots, but God has designed us to display the excellence of the power, or vigor, of God.

God gave you a body so He would have a container into which He could pour His Spirit. He wants to fill that earthen vessel not so it's just full, but so it's overflowing.

WE NEED TO TAKE A DIP IN THE HOLY GHOST

John the Baptist said, "I indeed baptize you with water unto repentance: but he that cometh after me is mightier than I, whose shoes I am not worthy to bear: he shall baptize you with the Holy Ghost, and with fire" (Matt. 3:11). John was saying, "If you think my baptism is good, wait until you get baptized with the Holy Ghost."

Baptism means "to immerse." It doesn't mean to sprinkle or pour; it means to jump in the river and splash around until you're soaking wet. What the body of Christ needs is an immersion in the Holy Ghost. It's time to take a dip!

When you're ready for a dip, you don't worry about your makeup or your hair color or your false eyelashes. When you take a dip, your dignity goes right along with you and washes off in the water.

But other things wash off as well: your sorrow, your discouragement, your bondage. Best of all, the water washes Old Man Religion away. And when you come up out of that water, you're a new creature. You're not immersed in the Holy Ghost for nothing.

If you want to take a dip, you have to determine that you don't care what you look like when you come out of the water. You don't care who likes you and who doesn't like you. You don't care what's around you. You don't care what people say about you. You just want to jump back in and take another dip.

Some people think one dip is all they need. The problem with that thinking is, when you jump into the water, your clothes get wet, but they eventually dry. Then you need to jump in again.

The apostle Paul exhorts us to "be filled with the Spirit" (Eph. 5:18). The term *filled* is a poor translation because it is rendered past tense, giving the idea that you only have to be filled once, thus inferring that after the action is completed, you're done. But the Greek word for "filled" isn't past tense, but present tense, meaning the action continues. In addition, the verb tense of the word is in the

imperative case, meaning that Paul's exhortation isn't just a sugges-
tion, it's a command. A more accurate translation would be "You
must be continuously filled with the Spirit."

People who say, "I don't need a dip," are easy to pick out of a
crowd. They're the ones with a sour face who constantly complain
and blame other people for why they're not blessed. They wear their
religiosity like a medal and gripe if they don't get their way. Of all
people, they need a dip!

No one is above needing a dip. If you don't speak in tongues as
much as you used to, you need a dip. If you're discouraged about
your business, take a dip. Are you worried about your children?
Take a dip. Every time sin comes knocking, you need to get on your
knees and take a dip. Whenever you sense fear trying to close in,
take a dip.

THE PURPOSE OF GOD'S PRESENCE
IS THE RELEASE OF HIS POWER

Aren't you tired of marking time and living in defeat? Jesus said, "But
ye shall receive power, after that the Holy Ghost is come upon you"
(Acts 1:8). The kind of power I'm talking about is: blind-eye healing
power, deaf-ear healing power and lame-man walking power!

When the Holy Ghost baptizes you, God incarnates you as He did
Gideon. You march with poise against an army of thousands when
you have an army of only three hundred. You radiate with confidence
because you know the vigor of the breaker is backing you up and
pushing you forward. You have nothing to fear because you know
God is fighting the battle for you. You're just going along for the ride.

The purpose of the baptism of the Holy Spirit is to release
God's power. Power to witness your family being saved and your
children healed. Power to see your bank account prosper. Power to
live above sin. Power to walk in health. Power to boldly proclaim the

gospel of Christ, which is the power of God unto salvation to every one who believeth.

THE FULLNESS OF THE SPIRIT WILL BE POURED OUT ON *ALL* FLESH

Quoting the prophet Joel, Peter proclaimed in Acts 2, "And it shall come to pass in the last days, saith God, I will pour out of my Spirit upon all flesh: and your sons and your daughters shall prophesy, and your young men shall see visions, and your old men shall dream dreams" (v. 17). The outpouring of God's Spirit is a sign of the last days.

Why is it that we hear preachers preach about the last days and we read books about the last days, but we don't hear much about prophetic utterances? Even Pentecostal preachers are hesitant to preach about the outpouring of the Holy Spirit. We're afraid to pray with people to receive the baptism of the Holy Spirit, and we're ashamed to speak with other tongues. Yet, as noted in Peter's proclamation above, the Spirit poured out on all flesh is a sign of the last days.

Look at yourself. Do you have flesh? Well, then, He's talking about you. God said He would pour out His Spirit on *all* flesh in the last days. The baptism of the Holy Spirit with the evidence of speaking in tongues is your divine right—just as it was to the New Testament church. The Spirit of the Lord can clothe you just as He did Gideon.

During the Feast of Pentecost, the believers gathered in one place seeking to obey Jesus' command to wait in Jerusalem until they were clothed with power from on high. Suddenly, a mighty, rushing wind filled the place and all the believers in the Upper Room began speaking with other tongues. "And they were *all* filled with the Holy Ghost, and began to speak with other tongues, as the Spirit gave them utterance" (Acts 2:4, italics added).

"Speaking with other tongues" means you are able to speak a language that you have never learned before. It may be an understandable language such as Spanish or French, but more often it is the language of the Spirit—your spirit communicating with the Holy Spirit.[2] You may have been told that only certain people can speak with other tongues, but when the Spirit of God was poured out on *all* flesh, *all* believers spoke in tongues. People who say, "I believe that tongues are real, but they just aren't for me" are usually people who have never sought God to receive this gift.

THE HOLY SPIRIT BYPASSES THE MIND BUT IS SUBJECT TO OUR WILL

Most people aren't baptized in the Holy Spirit with the evidence of speaking in tongues because they think too much. They either decide they don't need it or they ask but don't receive it. Their mind tells them speaking in tongues isn't normal. But since God's ways are higher than our ways (Isa. 55:9), the ways of the Spirit naturally transcend our mind. The mind is unable to understand the Spirit, so God gives us a means to bypass it. Paul wrote,

> I will pray with the spirit; and I will pray with the understanding also: I will sing with the spirit, and I will sing with the understanding also. (1 Cor. 14:15)

The mind isn't inherently evil; it just gets in the way sometimes.

When you're driving with your friends and you pass a car accident on the side of the road, you don't have to wonder, *What do I pray?* You pray in the Spirit. And if your friends tell you, "I think you've lost your mind," you just respond, "That's exactly right. I'm not dominated by my mind."

Notice that Paul wrote, "I *will* pray with the spirit, and I *will* pray with the understanding." Praying in the spirit and praying with the understanding are subject to our wills. The first time you speak in tongues, your mind will immediately tell you, *That's not it. You're just making it up.* But your immediate response to the devil should be, "Well, who do you think is doing it? Crazy devil, of course it's me."

The devil will do anything he can to keep you from praying in tongues because he has no defense against it. He can't understand tongues, so when your spirit partners with the Holy Spirit, he is rendered defenseless.

When you receive the baptism in the Holy Spirit, you are the one speaking in tongues, but it's the Holy Spirit giving you the words to say. He's not going to invade your body, push your diaphragm in and out, wiggle your tongue, and move your jaw. Some people think that if they're really filled with the Spirit of God, they just have to sit there and God is going to do all the work. Wrong. With your will you pray in the spirit and with your will you pray with understanding.

If you grew up with brothers or sisters, there were probably times as a child when your mother or father told you to find your sibling and tell him or her that it was time to eat. If you were an obedient child and actually relayed the message, who said it? You did. Who gave you the message? Your parent.

On Pentecost Sunday, the believers were "all filled with the Holy Ghost, and began to speak with other tongues, *as the Spirit gave them utterance*" (Acts 2:4, italics added). God fills us with His Spirit and the Spirit gives us the words as we make the willful decision to speak.

YOU CAN BE CLOTHED WITH POWER FROM ON HIGH RIGHT NOW

If you have never spoken in tongues or you haven't spoken in tongues in a long time, you can be filled with the Holy Ghost right now. Just lay your hands on your belly, because that's where your spirit lives, and pray this very simple prayer.

> *Lord Jesus Christ, I come to You today as a believer. You are my Savior and You are the Baptizer in the Holy Spirit. I ask You this day to baptize me in the Holy Spirit, clothe me with power from on high, and give me that heavenly language to speak mysteries and to glorify You. By faith I believe I am now baptized in the Holy Spirit. Thank You. Amen.*

You can now speak in that heavenly language as readily as you can speak in English. You can speak in tongues whenever you want and you can stop whenever you want. If you can't stop, it's not the Holy Spirit, because Paul said, "I will." You don't have to jump and yell and roll on the floor in order to receive the baptism of the Holy Ghost.

GIDEON WAS AN OLD TESTAMENT PENTECOSTAL!

Gideon didn't pray in tongues because the Spirit hadn't been fully given, but God clothed him with power and gave him the ability to rally the Israelite troops against the advancing armies. He was so successful at rallying the troops that he had too many men. So God told him, "Tell anyone who is fearful to go home." Two-thirds of the men immediately departed. But God said, "You still have too many men." Gideon pared the troops again until only 300 out of 32,000 men remained. Then God said, "With this remnant, you will witness My power at work."

The men divided themselves into three battalions of 100 and then surrounded their enemy in the late evening. In their hands they held trumpets *and clay jars with torches inside.* The glory of God was about to be revealed through jars of clay—both literally and figuratively. When Gideon gave the word, the men blew their trumpets and broke their lamps, startling the enemy troops. In their confusion, the troops began killing one another. That night and the following weeks, God defeated Israel's enemies and restored the people of Israel.

When you are clothed with power from on high, not only does God work in you, He works through you and around you. Through the baptism of the Holy Ghost, you are dressed for battle because you are clothed with Christ and empowered by the vigor of the breaker.

PART V

OVERPOWERING WEALTH: THE CAPACITY OF THE BREAKER

CHAPTER 13

HIDDEN RICHES,
EXTRAVAGANT WEALTH

During the early days of the Great Depression, a man named Ira Yates eked out a meager living on the wide expanse of the West Texas prairie. Although the ranch he owned was large, livestock prices were low and he was unable to pay the principal and interest on his mortgage. Watching his sheep graze on the rolling hills, he faced the real possibility that his ranch could be turned over to his creditors.

Unable to afford food or clothing for his family, Ira finally swallowed his pride and applied for government assistance.

Then one day a car drove onto the property, and a man in a fancy suit stepped out, looking for Yates. He represented an oil company and asked permission to drill a wildcat well on Yates's property. *What do I have to lose?* Ira thought. He signed a lease and the man drove away down the long, dusty road.

A few days later, an oil crew began setting up a rig on Yates's property. They drilled 500 feet down and found nothing. Then 800 feet. Nothing. 1,100 feet. Still no oil. But at 1,115 feet, the men struck an enormous oil reserve that eventually yielded an average of 80,000 barrels of liquid gold a day. Additional wells were soon drilled. Thirty years later a government test determined that each of the many wells could yield up to 125,000 barrels a day. This famous oil field, now known as Yates Pool, is one of the largest oil fields in the United States.

One day, Yates was living in utter poverty; the next day he was a multimillionaire. And really, he was a millionaire all along. He just didn't realize it.[1]

When you think about it, most Christians are just like the man in this true story. First, the riches God has in store for us have nothing to do with our effort. Yates simply allowed the oil company to drill for oil on the land he already possessed. Second, all Christians are rich; most just don't realize it. As a result, the majority of Christians are hindered by a poverty mentality. But most important, we, like Mr. Yates, possess a fortune that lies hidden. Our responsibility is to find it, or we will continue living in poverty.

The final quality of a breaker is overpowering wealth. The sons of Perez who rebuilt the walls of Jerusalem and then inhabited the Holy City were men of great financial means. They understood the importance of virtue, valor, and vigor, but they also understood the divine principles of overpowering wealth. In this last section, you will learn the biblical principles that will complete your transformation into a son or daughter of Perez.

Although some cannot even conceive the idea of becoming wealthy, it's much simpler than you would think. In fact, it begins much like Ira Yates—by doing nothing at all.

YOU ARE ALREADY ANOINTED

Thus saith the LORD to his anointed . . . (Isa. 45:1)

In this passage, Isaiah's prophecy was intended for King Cyrus. But as Christians we are *all* anointed, which means Isaiah's prophecy is intended for every Christian. John wrote, "But ye"—that means "you all"—"have an unction from the Holy One, and ye know all things" (1 John 2:20). Whenever you read about the anointing, or unction, in Scripture, pay close attention because that prophecy is intended specifically for you.

You don't have to try to get anointed. You don't have to wait until the right worship song is sung or get on your knees to be anointed. You don't have to perform any religious exercise to be anointed because you already *are* anointed.

Everything in your life doesn't have to be perfect for you to be anointed because your anointing is greater than any obstacle that comes against it. "But the anointing which ye have received of him abideth in you" (1 John 2:27). The burden-removing, yoke-destroying, devil-defeating anointing already lives within you. Your mind may not understand it, you may not feel it, but it has no bearing upon the reality of the anointing in your life.

God isn't revealing Himself to everyone in this late hour; He's only speaking to His anointed. The anointing, however, extends not only to those who speak, but also to those who listen. When I preach in church, not only do I need the anointing to speak God's words, but the people in my congregation also need the anointing to hear it.

You need the anointing to hear the word of the Lord; to receive revelation knowledge; to know what no one else knows; to hear what no one else hears; to see what no one else sees; and to feel what no one else feels. You need the anointing to break through any obstacle that stands in your way.

YOUR PROBLEM IS DESIGNED TO PROPEL YOU FROM WHERE YOU ARE TO WHERE GOD WANTS YOU TO BE

I will go before thee, and make the crooked places straight: I will break in pieces the gates of brass, and cut in sunder the bars of iron. (Isa. 45:2)

The prophet Isaiah saw a barrier between the anointed and God's provision: gates of brass and bars of iron. At that time, brass and iron were the two hardest metals. So together, they formed a barricade that seemed impossible to penetrate.

Believe it or not, your barrier is your benefit. Your problem is specifically designed by God to propel you from where you are to where He wants you to be. When the Israelites were backed up against the Red Sea with the Egyptian army quickly approaching, they saw a barrier. But God said, "I'm making a way through." What they saw as the *end,* God saw as the beginning of victory.

God's purpose is to push you into the walk of faith so you will accomplish mighty feats of virtue, valor, vigor, and overpowering wealth beyond your wildest dreams.

Our natural tendency is to rely on our mental and physical prowess to work ourselves out of any sticky situation. But God is going to allow you to fall on your face so that you will realize that you cannot rely on yourself. "For it is God which worketh in you both to will and to do of his good pleasure" (Phil. 2:13). As you step aside and let God lead the way, you will break through any obstacle that stands before you.

You may be facing a problem that you are certain is going to crush you and keep you from entering the promised land. But I have good news for you: God is going to use that very situation to propel you into a dimension of the anointing that you never realized was possible.

In Isaiah 51:10, God said, "Art thou not it which hath dried the sea, the waters of the great deep; that hath made the depths of the sea a way for the ransomed to pass over?" You're about to pass over the very thing that you've been looking at and saying, "I'll never survive." You just stand still a minute, and God is going to make a way for you to pass.

GOD KNOWS THE WAY BECAUSE
HE'S BEEN THERE BEFORE YOU

In Isaiah's prophecy, God said, "I will go before thee." If God is going before you, then you can't go anywhere that He hasn't been. No matter how hopeless your situation, no matter how bleak your prognosis, He's already been there.

Have you ever considered how silly it is to pray, "Lord God, would You come and bless us with Your presence?" God is already there because He is omnipresent. The Bible tells us that God "filleth all in all" (Eph. 1:23). If He isn't there already, then where would He come from? He was there when you arrived and when you leave, He will still be there.

When Shadrach, Meshach, and Abednego were thrown into the fiery furnace, the fourth man, the one like unto the Son of man, didn't jump in after He heard they were in trouble. He was already there, waiting for them. Right in the middle of the fire, right in the middle of the flood, right in the middle of your mess, God Almighty is already waiting for you. "I will go before thee, and make the crooked places straight: I will break in pieces the gates of brass, and cut in sunder the bars of iron."

In the same way that God is already waiting for you, the devil is waiting for you as well. He tells you that you're not good enough, that you're not smart enough, that you'll never break through the gates of brass and bars of iron that imprison you. But when you hear his voice, you know it's not the time to be cute or pretty. It's time to push everybody and everything out of your way.

God has a plan to break through the financial barriers that prevent you from propagating the gospel and accomplishing His will here on earth. If you don't have the anointed ears to hear, somebody else may take your portion—and it might as well be me! Even if I have to push you out of my way and get all sweaty and shout my hair down, I'll do it in order to get what God said I can have.

When Tamar was giving birth to her twin sons, Zerah stuck his arm out first. But Perez wasn't about to let his brother muscle in on his birthright. The midwife tied a scarlet cord around the infant Zerah's arm, but soon the arm disappeared and shortly thereafter, Perez was born. The difference between Perez and his slightly younger brother Zerah is that Perez was fiercely determined to have what belonged to him (see Gen. 38:27–30).

TREASURES IN DARKNESS, HIDDEN RICHES IN SECRET

And I will give thee the treasures of darkness, and hidden riches of secret places, that thou mayest know that I, the LORD, which call thee by thy name, am the God of Israel. (Isa. 45:3)

The gates of brass and bars of iron prevent God's anointed people from discovering the overpowering wealth that is the birthright of the breaker. Every Christian is anointed to break through, but few ever accomplish it. Like Ira Yates, many live in poverty while sitting on their reserves.

But those who kick down the barriers discover wealth beyond imagination. You probably didn't know that treasures and riches are hidden just beyond your grasp. You can reap where you haven't sowed. You can make withdrawals from an account that you have never deposited money in. You can drill for oil on land that doesn't even belong to you.

A barrier may exist between you and overpowering wealth, but God has gone before you to make a way through. He makes the crooked places straight, He dries the sea, He makes a way in the wilderness. He drills the well and gives you the profits.

God has gone before you to make a way to the treasures He has stored just for you. You see, God left wealth for you that you're on the brink of discovering. Wealth that you didn't earn or deserve. Wealth that you have never seen or touched.

> But as it is written, Eye hath not seen, nor ear heard, neither have entered into the heart of man, the things which God hath prepared for them that love him. (1 Cor. 2:9)

Before the oil company drilled for oil, Ira Yates couldn't imagine the wealth in store for him. God isn't going before you to politely knock on the gate of brass. He isn't going before you to test the iron bars and see how sturdy they are. God is going before you to kick down the gate, stretch wide the iron bars, and lead you into treasures of darkness and hidden riches in secret places.

GOD IS GOING TO PUT INTO YOUR HANDS THE MEANS TO ACCOMPLISH HIS PURPOSES

As I mentioned earlier in this book, God's reason for inundating you with wealth is not so you can spend it extravagantly on meaningless things. God uses people to accomplish His purposes, and He blesses you with the provision to make it happen.

Abraham was promised, "I will bless thee, and make thy name great; and thou shalt be a blessing" (Gen. 12:2). The blessing starts with us but certainly doesn't end with us. We are channels of God's blessing and the vehicle that accomplishes His will.

Extravagant wealth is going to be poured into our laps so we can send missionaries throughout the world to share the good news of Jesus Christ. We will be blessed with an overflow of abundance so we can purchase commercial time on the major television networks and preach the gospel. The day is coming when the church will be able to pay for five minutes of airtime during the Super Bowl half-time show so a captive audience will hear that Jesus is still the answer for every situation that plagues humanity.

The Bible tells us, "And God is able to make all grace abound toward you; that ye, always having all sufficiency in all things, may abound to every good work" (2 Cor. 9:8). If you have the faith to believe, God has the wealth available to make you a channel of blessing to the whole world.

GOD RESERVED THE WEALTH FOR YOU BECAUSE HE KNEW OTHERS WOULDN'T USE IT RIGHT

Treasures in darkness and hidden riches are earmarked for a specific people who are prophetically equipped to find them. The people in Isaiah's prophecy were anointed for the express purpose of discovering riches. Did you know that you were anointed to find and accumulate wealth?

The wealth is hidden because God knows many Christians won't use it the way God originally intended. James 4:3 says, "Ye ask, and receive not, because ye ask amiss, that ye may consume it upon your lusts." Seeking God to satisfy your lusts is a sure way to continue hunting for those treasures in darkness. But if God can pour the wealth into the hands of His anointed, He'll have a people with the provision to preach the gospel and perpetuate His plan on the earth.

Now you may be reading this book and saying to yourself, *I don't quite understand what he's talking about. I'm anointed to find money?* Well, yes and no. Not everyone is anointed to hear this message. But if something went off in your spirit while you were reading this and you said, "Yes sir, that's me," then I'm writing to you. You're anointed to find treasures in darkness and hidden riches.

GOD IS GOING TO BREAK THROUGH
YOUR POVERTY MENTALITY

God is going to go before you and break through the gates of brass and bars of iron. By the power of the Holy Spirit of God you are going to have a breakthrough, a sudden burst of advanced knowledge of God.

Once and for all, you are going to break through that poverty mentality that separates you from God's blessing. You're going to obliterate the welfare mind-set that says, "I don't have enough, and I will never amount to anything."

You're going to square your shoulders and speak to your lack saying, "God Almighty has revealed unto me by His Spirit what the eye cannot see, what the ear cannot hear, and what the mind cannot comprehend. And because He is going before me, God is breaking down the impenetrable barriers that stand in my way. Divine revelation is illuminating my steps, the darkness is now revealed, and I can see the treasure He has left behind for me. Treasures in darkness and hidden riches in the secret places are mine. I'm breaking through!"

> But thou shalt remember the LORD thy God: for it is he that giveth thee power to get wealth, that he may establish his covenant which he sware unto thy fathers, as it is this day. (Deut. 8:18)

Some people believe that their ability to make money gives them the right to spend what they earn on whatever they desire. But even *that* ability doesn't belong to them. Because it comes from God, it belongs to God.

But knowing that the power to get wealth comes from God means Christians who aren't wealthy can be wealthy, too. No Christian is ever without hope! God cut a covenant with Abraham in Genesis 12, and then continually reminded him of it throughout Abraham's life, promising to bless him, his descendants, and all the families of the earth (see Gen. 13:16; 15:5; 17:5–6; 18:17–18; 22:17–18). As spiritual heirs of Abraham, we can remind God of the covenant He made with our spiritual father, Abraham.

GOD IS JUST USING YOU

God has chosen you to finance the work of the kingdom. Not long ago someone walked up to me and handed me a tithe check numbering in the tens of thousands of dollars. A tithe check! God kept His part of the covenant to bless her, and she kept her part by funneling it through.

Some people say, "God could never bless me—look at the job I work at. Look at the skeletons hiding in my closet. I don't have the ability or confidence. Maybe He could use someone else, but He surely couldn't use me." Well it's not about you.

Have you ever been in a relationship where you felt that you were being used? Perhaps a person of the opposite sex wanted your money or pretended to like you in order to make another person jealous? Maybe your friends even pulled you aside and said, "She's just using you," or "He's just using you."

Can I let you in on a secret? *God is just using you!* And He's going to use you up. If you have the fearless courage of the breaker to pray, "Use me, Lord," then watch out, because He will answer your prayer. God covenanted with Abraham to bless all the families of the earth and to make His name great among *all* people. He's looking for people through whom He will finance the final great outpouring of His Spirit, which will usher in the end of the age. But He needs people who will come into agreement with Him and allow Him to work through them.

GET READY FOR THE GREAT TRANSFER OF WEALTH INTO THE REMNANT'S HANDS

Men and women endowed with the spirit of the breaker are propelled by a power greater than themselves. They're compelled to serve an infallible leader with irresistible power based on absolute truth. God is going to place you in impossible situations. He is going to allow you to be encased by gates of brass and bars of iron so that you and all those around you will know that God is the one who delivers you. He is determined to bring glory and honor to His name.

An overwhelming transfer of wealth into the hands of remnant believers is about to take place before the eyes of the world. And those with the anointed ears to hear will become overpoweringly mighty by reason of their wealth.

Eventually, the world is going to have to deal with us. They've ignored us and shoved us aside, but before we exit this temporal world by way of the Rapture, we're taking over. The politicians and world leaders are going to have to deal with us. The media are going to have to deal with us. We are breakers!

GOD IS GOING TO USE YOU TO SHAKE THE FOUNDATIONS OF THE EARTH WITH THE GOSPEL

When God first called me to start World Harvest Church, it was hard to get a loan from a bank to build our first church building. All we needed was $85,000 for the land and the building—and that was nearly twenty-five years ago. So I, my family, and some of those who were with me at that time set out to do whatever we had to do in order to give above and beyond what we could normally give. We were faithful in applying biblical principles to our finances, and now banks call us every day asking to give us a loan. Not long ago a bank called our ministry asking if we would like to have a million-dollar line of credit.

My answer was an emphatic no, but the fact is, I couldn't beg, plead, borrow, and steal to get a small loan from them just a few years ago. Now they want to loan me a million dollars.

Not long ago a major company decided to sow $100,000 into our ministry. What kind of God do we serve? The God of hidden riches and extravagant wealth who is committed to using us to shake the foundations of the earth for the gospel.

Those are just two small examples of what is about to take place. When the wealth of the world is transferred into the hands of the anointed breakers, it is going to happen fast and furiously.

In the next chapter I am going to share with you in greater detail how God blessed our ministry so you can know how to apply these biblical principles to your life and ministry.

CHAPTER 14

ANOINTED PREACHERS, ANOINTED PEOPLE, AND ABUNDANT PROVISION

In 1977, a passionate twenty-year-old man prayed, "God, please do things so incredibly large and powerful through this ministry that people will have to look past me to You and say, 'No person could have done this.'" I was young and inexperienced enough to believe God would answer my prayer. And He did.

Twenty-four years later I look at how God turned a Bible study of seventeen people into a church of twelve thousand in attendance weekly, and I marvel. Only God could have done this!

As I mentioned in the last chapter, God is looking for people endowed with the spirit of the breaker through whom He can perpetrate His purposes. In this chapter I am going to share a little bit of the World Harvest story and the biblical principles that have guided us into realms of blessing beyond anything that I could have imagined.

IN THE BEGINNING . . .

Before our *Breakthrough* television ministry had gone worldwide, before there was a World Harvest Bible College, even before filling our present 5,200-seat sanctuary, there was a young preacher living in a little one-bedroom bachelor apartment on East Main Street in Columbus, Ohio. All I had in my room was an old, worn-out rocker-recliner, a tiny television sitting on an orange crate, and a metal TV tray that I used for a desk. The year was 1986.

Despite moving into a new facility, our church lacked adequate office space. So I sat in my little apartment while the Holy Ghost dealt with me about the need to build an office complex. The vision was there, but the finances were not.

"I know what You're calling me to do," I told God. "But I cannot do it with the finances that are coming into this ministry. I've been a tither."

Very quietly God answered, "No you haven't."

I was taken aback by His response. "Now wait just one minute. I have always given You 10 percent. Ever since my mama and daddy gave me my first allowance of 50 cents and kept back a nickel, I have been a tither. They told me, 'The tithe belongs to God; don't ever touch it.' And I haven't. Not once in my life have I received a dollar bill that I didn't pay my tithe on."

But God said again, "You're not tithing."

We went back and forth for a while, but I knew that our discussion was futile. When you say something to God and God responds, and then you answer back but this time He doesn't respond, then you know you missed it. I wasn't about to let that happen, so I listened.

GOD GAVE HIS BEST, SO WE SHOULD GIVE HIM OUR BEST

That day, sitting on my old recliner with my Bible opened up on my TV-tray desk, God dropped a word into my spirit that changed my life:

I'm going to give you a key. Every spring, you tell your congregation that Easter is the time when I gave My best by bolting My only Son, Jesus, to the rugged, cruel cross of Calvary and shedding His spotless blood. I gave My best; now tell your congregation that at this time every year, they should give their best. All year long you and your people give 10 percent, and live on 90 percent. From this point forward, on the day you celebrate Easter, ask the people to give Me one week's income.

That day I committed myself to working as hard as I could the two weeks leading up to Easter, preaching in crusades around the country and giving all the proceeds to God. The offering we would receive on Easter Sunday would be called our "resurrection seed" because Jesus was God's resurrection seed. After being nailed to the cross, He died and was buried in the ground, but after three days, He rose from the dead, conquering death, disease, and hell.

The next Sunday I told my congregation—they were just a fraction of our congregation now—that God promised to give us a $100,000 cash offering on Easter morning and that the greatest breakthrough miracles of their lives would transpire as a result of them giving their best. "And with our $100,000 resurrection seed offering," I promised, "we're going to build an office building on our property and pay cash for it." After I challenged the congregation, they looked back in disbelief.

Every week leading up to Easter, I preached it to my congregation and inwardly I prayed, *Lord, help them get it.*

YOU CAN OVERTAKE THE DEVOURER THROUGH GIVING

One man told me, "Pastor, you need to quit preaching that resurrection seed message. Ever since you started talking about giving

God 100 percent the week of Easter, I've been tormented with the same terrible dream every night. In my dream, a horrible monster appears inside the church building and says, 'If you don't stop preaching that stuff, I'm going to devour the whole ministry.' God's trying to tell you through my dream that if you don't stop it, it's gonna kill the church."

After listening to the man I told him, "Brother, I don't doubt that you had a dream, but why don't you go back to your knees and pray for the interpretation."

The next Sunday in church the man whom I had spoken to just a week earlier came walking hurriedly down the aisle to where I was standing. "Pastor, Pastor, I gotta tell you something. God gave me the interpretation of my dream. Here's what He said: 'It's not Pastor Parsley's preaching that is producing that monster. The monster has been there all along devouring the people's harvest. And the more Pastor Parsley preaches it, the more that monster is revealed.'" He then said, "Pastor Parsley, please don't stop preaching that message!"

There is a way to break through your lack. The devourer is intent on consuming everything you have. But when you release your best into the kingdom, God brings an overflow of abundance into your life. See, the key to keeping the devourer from getting your stuff isn't by hanging on to it. The key is in releasing it into the kingdom of God.

GOD WAS SETTING THE STAGE FOR A MIRACLE

And the faith of the people began to grow. I'm an audience participation preacher, so on Sunday mornings I would ask the congregation to repeat after me, "God's gonna give us a $100,000 offering." At first only a few would respond. The next week I would ask them to say, "God's gonna give us a miracle." A few more would respond.

Over the next few weeks, the people's faith began to rise up.

Anticipation began to build among the congregation as we wondered what God was going to accomplish.

On Easter morning I stepped onto the platform during worship, looked into the congregation, and saw a television camera stationed in one of the aisles. It wasn't like the ones we were using; it was a real TV camera. *Dear God, the miracle has already started!* I thought.

As I surveyed the congregation further, I discovered that another television station was covering our service, too. Someone had called the local network affiliates reporting that a crazy bunch of Christians were believing that God would give them a $100,000 miracle. "That church is just a bunch of farmers and laborers," the networks were told. "There's nobody rich there. How in the name of God are they going to raise $100,000?" But little is much when God is in it.

During that Easter service I realized the networks had shown up to see what God *wasn't* going to do. I stepped off the platform and politely showed the camera technicians where to station their cameras. Then I gathered some of my key ministry team members together and told them, "After we receive this offering, you go into the back room and count it and when you're finished, bring a report into the service. I'm gonna tell them what God did." We brought our resurrection seed to God, and then I commenced preaching.

That morning I preached as if the Rapture were going to occur in the middle of the service. I preached and I preached and then I waited and I waited. Finally I called an usher to the front and told him, "Go into the back room and tell the people counting the money to bring me a report *right now*." He did as I asked and shortly thereafter he returned.

As he walked up the aisle and onto the platform, the usher was shaking his head. My sister, who was sitting on the second row, saw the look on his face and immediately sat down, put her head between her knees and prayed, "Dear God, for the first time in his life, let my preacher brother lie. Just let him tell them it was $100,000 no matter what came in the offering. We'll repent later. Don't make a fool out of us."

"Come here," I called to him. "Why are you shaking your head?"

"The door was locked," he answered. "I couldn't get in."

"Well, then you kick the door down," I replied.

About that time Mary, a dear lady in our church who is like a grandmother to me, came running through the door with a little strip of adding machine paper in her hand. She waved the paper in the air as she came down the aisle and then handed it to me.

I read the piece of paper and then I looked into the TV cameras. "You news channels, listen here," I began. "God's about to use us as a sign and a wonder because He didn't give us $100,000 or $110,000 or $120,000 or 130 or 140. God gave us a $147,000 miracle today." The congregation erupted in applause and rose to their feet.

THE RESURRECTION SEED IS ANOINTED SEED

Every Easter Sunday, since that day in 1986 when our congregation sowed their resurrection seed, we join together in agreement with one another and the Word of God, believing that God is going to loose the chains of poverty and lack from our lives. We believe that just as Jesus broke through the tomb on the third day, the resurrection seeds we sow will break through any financial barriers that stand in our way.

Since that day our congregation has experienced breakthrough after breakthrough. Countless men and women have been delivered from bondage to the spirit of this world, which is lack and debt, and into financial freedom as a result of the supernatural power of God.

A powerful anointing of God rests on the resurrection seed. And when we give God our best, just as He gave His best when He sent Jesus to die for our sins, we are empowered with the spirit of the breaker to overtake the enemy, to overthrow his kingdom, and to overflow in the abundance of God.

GOD'S VISION FOR THE WORLD IS SALVATION

Where there is no vision, the people perish. (Prov. 29:18)

As we learned in the last chapter, God's treasures are masked in darkness, and His riches are hidden in the secret places. In order to find them, we need a vision from God.

The word *vision* used in Proverbs 29:18 is not the best translation. Other versions of the Bible more accurately translate the word as "revelation" or even "prophetic unction." Where there is no fresh "now" word of God, anointed and energized by the Holy Spirit, the people will die.

Vision has become a misunderstood, overused word. Books extol the virtue of vision. Pastors preach on the importance of vision. Yet the vision of most people begins and ends with them.

Vision isn't starting a church, growing a congregation, and buying a Mercedes. Vision isn't getting your picture on the cover of a Christian magazine. Vision is this:

> For God so loved the world, that he gave his only begotten Son, that whosoever believeth in him should not perish, but have everlasting life. For God sent not his Son into the world to condemn the world; but that the world through him might be saved. (John 3:16–17)

You see, vision and the fruit of vision—overpowering wealth—have everything to do with the resurrection seed, Jesus Christ. The salvation of the world is God's vision, and His vision has never changed.

God gives us a vision and then He gives us the power to get

wealth (Deut. 8:18). Why? So He can establish His covenant on the earth through us. Think about these questions for a moment:

- Do you believe that God is not willing that any should perish, but that all should come to repentance? (See 2 Peter 3:9.)

- Do you believe that it is God's will that this gospel of the kingdom shall be preached in all the world for a witness unto all nations; and then the end shall come? (See Matt. 24:14.)

- Do you believe that Jesus came to seek and to save that which was lost? (See Luke 19:10.)

- Do you believe that He came to give His life a ransom for many? (See Mark 10:45.)

- Do you believe that we definitely will win in the end? (See Rev. 20:11–15.)

- Do you believe that entire nations are going to flow into the kingdom of God? (See Rev. 15:4.)

If you believe the answer to the questions above is yes, that God's kingdom *will* come and His will *will* be done, then you must also believe that it will take place according to His Word. And, according to God's Word, He is going to bless you with the power to get wealth so you can release those funds into the kingdom and the gospel can be preached.

Vision propels God's wealth machine in motion. However, vision is usually hard to find. So, where does vision begin?

WE NEED AN ANOINTED MAN OF GOD

Where there is no prophetic word, the people cast off all restraint. They run wild. In other words, people without vision lack the means to come together in agreement. They run in different directions and pray for different needs. As a result, they're powerless. What they need is an anointed man of God.

Now, if people want an anointed vision from God, they're first going to have to call on Him. "Call unto me, and I will answer thee, and shew thee great and mighty things, which thou knowest not" (Jer. 33:3). But according to Romans 10:14, we cannot call until we have first believed, and we cannot believe until we have heard, and we cannot hear without a preacher.

> How then shall they call on him in whom they have not believed?
> and how shall they believe in him of whom they have not heard?
> and how shall they hear without a preacher? (Rom. 10:14)

According to God's Word, then, vision begins with one person who then imparts it to the congregation. And the people are blessed. Sitting on that worn-out recliner in my one-bedroom bachelor apartment on East Main Street in Columbus, Ohio, the Holy Ghost imparted to me a vision from God, a prophetic unction, for my church: "I gave the best; now I want you to celebrate it by giving your best, once a year." And our congregation has walked in blessing because of it.

Repeatedly in Scripture, the people of Israel persecuted their prophets and God judged them for it. But believing the anointed word of the prophet is a key to God's blessing:

> Believe in the LORD your God, so shall ye be established; believe
> his prophets, so shall ye prosper. (2 Chron. 20:20)

When God Almighty anoints a man and that man begins to speak the anointed words of God, the people hear that word. And when the people hear that word, they believe it and come into agreement with it. Then they can call, and when they call, God answers and His power is released.

Nothing will stop the anointing of the Holy Ghost quicker than when a pastor is in disagreement with his congregation or when a congregation rebels against their pastor. If you want poverty in your church, then let rebellion flourish unrestrained.

PROVISION AND PROTECTION MAKE A FATHER

For though ye have ten thousand instructors in Christ, yet have ye not many fathers: for in Christ Jesus I have begotten you through the gospel. (1 Cor. 4:15)

A man is not a father simply because he can make babies. A man becomes a father when he takes responsibility for the provision and protection of those in his house. But he doesn't execute his duties haphazardly; he uses a plan. You're a father because you have a plan to protect and provide for those in your house.

Paul wrote to the church in Corinth that they had many instructors, but few fathers—men with a plan or a vision—to provide the spiritual nourishment and protection the people needed.

THOSE WHO DO NOT PROVIDE ARE WORSE THAN AN INFIDEL

But if any provide not for his own, and specially for those of his own house, he hath denied the faith, and is worse than an infidel. (1 Tim. 5:8)

An infidel is a person who is ruled by his senses: what he can see, what he can hear, what he can taste, what he can touch, what he can feel. So what is worse than being an infidel? Trying to rule your house by your senses. Unfortunately, this is the case in many churches, and for this reason many of our churches are powerless and poverty-stricken.

We need anointed preachers who are filled with the Spirit of God. Men of virtue, valor, and vigor who seek to be vessels of God's overpowering wealth. Men of vision, provision, and protection who hear God's voice, impart it with accuracy and the anointing, and who will fight on behalf of their own.

We need people with anointed ears to hear what God is saying through His prophets. Men and women who will gather around the vision, believe God's Word, and act on it.

As I think back on what God has brought World Harvest Church and me through, I truly have to say that no person could have done this. I don't claim to be the perfect pastor, but I seek an ever-increasing vision from God and I do my best to protect and provide for the people in my congregation.

The people at World Harvest Church, on the other hand, have anointed ears to hear what this man of God has to say. They have gathered around the vision, believed God's Word, and acted on it. And because of this, God has blessed us with abundance.

God is waiting to propel you into overpowering wealth. As you are faithful to be obedient in your giving unto Him, He will be faithful to break you through into abundant provision for your life.

CHAPTER 15

THE GREAT TRANSFER

I'm tired of seeing the wicked wallowing in wealth while believers are begging and borrowing to break even. I'm tired of seeing pornographers drive fancy cars while Christians drive around in jalopies held together with Christian bumper stickers. I'm tired of not being able to finance the spread of the gospel around the world.

Not long from now we're going to leave this temporal world. And if the Rapture is on its way, then the worldwide transfer of wealth from the hands of the wicked into the hands of the just will soon be upon us. The gospel of the kingdom will soon be preached in all the world for a witness and then the end will come (see Matt. 24:14). But first, the church has to learn the biblical principles of handling overpowering wealth.

THE WORLD'S SYSTEM IS BUILT ON LACK SPONSORED BY DEBT

The world's economic system is built on lack sponsored by debt. Yet debt is a curse. Proverbs 22:7 says, "The rich ruleth over the poor, and the borrower is servant to the lender." Christians shouldn't be bowing their knees to anyone but their heavenly Father.

Debt is devious because it is rooted in greed. Many folks are in financial bondage because they cannot resist the spirit of the world, which tells them they can have more—even if they cannot afford it. And really, greed is the spirit of the devil because it was he who said,

> For thou hast said in thine heart, I will ascend into heaven, I will exalt my throne above the stars of God: I will sit also upon the mount of the congregation, in the sides of the north: I will ascend above the heights of the clouds; I will be like the most High. (Isa. 14:13–14)

Five times in the two verses above, the word *I* is used. Greed says, "I am solely concerned with me." So the spirit of greed is the spirit of the world, which sponsors debt, which sponsors lack. You do not have that spirit.

A spirit of greed may be erected in front of you like a gate of brass and a bar of iron, but you are anointed to break through. Acts 10:38 says, "God anointed Jesus of Nazareth with the Holy Ghost and with power: who went about doing good, and healing all that were oppressed of the devil; for God was with him." If Jesus was anointed with a burden-removing, yoke-destroying, devil-defeating anointing and you are created in His image, then you are anointed with the burden-removing, yoke-destroying, devil-defeating anointing, too.

IT'S TIME FOR A REVOLUTIONARY UPRISING AGAINST THE SPIRIT OF DEBT

The time is ripe for a revolutionary uprising against the spirit of debt. It's about time we overthrow and overtake our adversary, seize what belongs to him, make it our own, and overflow in the abundance of God. We've been running from the adversary too long; now is the time to turn the tables.

This revolution isn't for everybody, but it is for somebody. It's for people who are tired of lack. People who are tired of not having enough food at home for their babies. People who are tired of the welfare mentality in our society. People who are tired of sitting at the back of the bus.

The revolution that is about to take place will be led by breakers who are willing to stand up and be counted, speak loudly to be heard, put their foot down, push their plate back, point their finger under the nose of the devil, and shout as loud as they can, "Enough is enough! I'm tired of this."

THE TIME HAS COME TO INSTALL GOD'S RIGHTEOUS GOVERNMENT

The dictionary defines *revolution* as "the overthrow or renunciation of one government or ruler and the substitution of another by the governed."[1] When a government fails to act in the best interests of the people it seeks to govern, it forfeits its rights to govern. We know that the government of this present age is bankrupt and acts only in its own best interests; therefore it holds no rights over the people it oppresses.

> And the seventh angel sounded; and there were great voices in heaven, saying, The kingdoms of this world are become the kingdoms of our Lord, and of his Christ; and he shall reign for ever and ever. (Rev. 11:15)

Because Jesus, the Breaker who goes before us, defeated death, destruction, and debt on the cross, we have the power and the God-given right to substitute the government of this world with the government of our Lord, and of His Christ.

WE OVERTHROW THIS WORLD'S ECONOMIC SYSTEM BY GIVING

If debt is a characteristic of this world's bankrupt economic system, then we overthrow it by acting in the opposite spirit. "Give, and it shall be given unto you; good measure, pressed down, and shaken together, and running over, shall men give into your bosom" (Luke 6:38).

If you want to change your financial situation, don't borrow—give, and God will give back to you in increasing measure. It's time to let go of what's in your hand so God will let go of what's in His. This is the anointed word of God, communicated to you by an anointed man of God. Now it is your responsibility to act on it.

When Israel was in economic ruin due to a severe drought, Elijah visited the widow at Zarephath and asked her to give him all the food she had—which amounted to only a handful of meal and a little oil in a jug. And as long as she supplied Elijah's needs with what little she had, God continued supplying her needs out of the abundance that He had. While the rest of Israel was starving, the widow at Zarephath enjoyed a steady supply of food.

THE BREAKER IS MAKING A WAY FOR YOU TO PASS THROUGH

Regardless of the lack you may be experiencing in your life, you are never beyond the reach of God's generous hand. When the children of Israel were carried into captivity, God raised up a prophet named Micah who prophesied that a Breaker was going before them and that through Him they would break through:

The breaker is come up before them: they have broken up, and have passed through the gate, and are gone out by it: and their king shall pass before them, and the LORD on the head of them. (Mic. 2:13)

Notice how similar Micah's prophecy is to Isaiah's:

I will go before thee, and make the crooked places straight: I will break in pieces the gates of brass, and cut in sunder the bars of iron. (Isa. 45:2)

Incidentally, Isaiah's and Micah's ministries coincided with each other. They looked at the degree of lack among their people and knew there was only one solution: an overthrow led by the Breaker who goes before us.

Some of you reading this book are headed toward gates of brass and bars of iron that you didn't know were there. Perhaps you already feel trapped by them. But God has a word for you: Don't worry about the bills that are due this week. Don't allow your bank account's bottom line to upset you. You're going to face some kind of obstacle. A tire may blow out on your car, but don't worry about it because, Jesus Christ, our Breaker, has gone before you, and you *will* break through behind Him.

EVEN IN CAPTIVITY GOD'S PEOPLE CAN'T GET IT RIGHT

One hundred fifty years later God again spoke into His people's lack:

Moreover the word of the LORD came unto me, saying, Son of man, when the house of Israel dwelt in their own land, they defiled it by their own way and by their doings: their way was

> before me as the uncleanness of a removed woman. Wherefore I poured my fury upon them for the blood that they had shed upon the land, and for their idols wherewith they had polluted it. (Ezek. 36:16–18)

The people of Judah defiled themselves because they shed innocent blood, worshiped idols, and touched the things that were sanctified for God's holy purposes. For these reasons God scattered them in hopes that they would see the seriousness of their sin and return to Him.

> And when they entered unto the heathen, whither they went, they profaned my holy name, when they said to them, These *are* the people of the LORD, and are gone forth out of his land. (Ezek. 36:20)

Despite being sent into captivity, Israel's sin continued. Their location changed but their behavior remained the same. Imagine God's frustration with His chosen people. "I brought you into a land flowing with milk and honey and you defiled it. Then I scattered you among the heathen, and you polluted My name there too."

Now imagine what the heathen nations thought: *These are the people of the most high God? Is this is the best they can do? Why, this ragtag bunch can't even keep their bills paid. This sick, broken-down, distressed, anxious, nervous, fearful bunch is the representation of God?*

GOD ALONE CAN DELIVER

This is a picture of the church. Our lives appear no different from the heathen world around us. We're drowning in debt, swamped in sin, and dying of disease. The apostle Paul described people like this as having a form of godliness but denying the power thereof (see 2 Tim. 3:5). His advice? Have nothing to do with them. And the world doesn't. Why would they want anything the church has to offer when we portray a powerless gospel? At least the world doesn't lay claim to the power of God. We do and have nothing to show for it.

God then took matters into His own hands.

> A new heart also will I give you, and a new spirit will I put within you: and I will take away the stony heart out of your flesh, and I will give you an heart of flesh. (Ezek. 36:26)

God said, "I'm tired of you making Me look bad. All you've done is mess it up. I'm through waiting for you to bring honor to My name because it may never happen. Instead of waiting, *I'm* going to retrieve the honor of My name and transform this motley-looking mess into a mighty army. What I am about to perform will have very little to do with you and everything to do with Me."

In these last days, God is preparing to transfer His overpowering wealth into the breakers' hands. Fortunately for us, God isn't looking for ability; He's looking for availability. He's not looking for perfection; He's looking for people who will passionately pursue Him. We don't have to beg, plead, borrow, and steal for God to bless us. God said, "I'm going to supernaturally place wealth in the lives of My people so that the world will look at them and say, 'It had to be God. It couldn't have been them because they're not smart enough.'" Now how does *that* make you feel?

Besides, we would never be worthy enough for God to bless us based on our own merit. Jesus said, "My grace is sufficient for thee: for my strength is made perfect in weakness" (2 Cor. 12:9). God has no intentions of sharing the credit, since everything we have comes from Him.

GOD IS GOING TO BLESS YOU FOR JESUS' SAKE

In order to bring about a revolution in your life against the spirit of lack and debt, you need to know what a revolution literally means: to return to the starting point. The earth takes 365 and a fraction days to revolve around the sun. Every year, then, the earth returns to its starting point.

If the devil has stolen from you, then God is going to return you to your starting point. Restoration is on the way! God promised us, "And I will restore to you the years that the locust hath eaten, the cankerworm, and the caterpiller, and the palmerworm, my great army which I sent among you" (Joel 2:25). God is going to restore everything the devil has stolen.

Because of his royal bloodline, Mephibosheth grew up enjoying the privileges of royalty. He ate from the king's table and dressed in royal attire. But after the death of his father, Jonathan, and his grandfather King Saul, Mephibosheth was forced to move out of the royal palace and learn to content himself eating crumbs and wearing rags. But God had a better idea and enacted a supernatural revolution in Mephibosheth's life.

You see, earlier, Jonathan and David, the eventual king of Israel, entered a covenant with one another. When King David realized that his dear deceased friend Jonathan had an heir, David sought out Mephibosheth and moved him back into the royal palace. Everything that was lost was restored. Mephibosheth ate once again from the king's table and was clothed in royal attire.

Most amazing is the fact that the covenant David enforced had nothing to do with Mephibosheth. David delivered Mephibosheth for Jonathan's sake. And do you know why God is going to bring a financial revolution in your life? Not for your sake. He's going to do it to retrieve the honor of His own holy name and for Jesus' sake, with whom you entered a covenant when you gave your life to Him. Our God is a covenant-keeping God.

TREASURE IS BEING STORED FOR THE LAST DAYS

> Go to now, ye rich men, weep and howl for your miseries that shall come upon you. Your riches are corrupted, and your garments are motheaten. Your gold and silver is cankered; and the rust of them shall be a witness against you, and shall eat your flesh as it were fire. Ye have heaped treasure together for the last days. (James 5:1–3)

James condemned the rich for amassing their fortunes and believing their wealth could offer them security. "Your efforts are in vain," he told them, "because your wealth is going to be used for a different purpose in the last days." Someone else would be spending the money the rich had accumulated.

> Be patient therefore, brethren, unto the coming of the Lord. Behold, the husbandman waiteth for the precious fruit of the earth, and hath long patience for it, until he receive the early and latter rain. (James 5:7)

The day of the latter rain has come, and the overpowering wealth that is stored up for the righteous is ready to be transferred into your hands. The people who have learned the importance of investing in the kingdom of God are positioned to receive this end-time harvest. God is about to unlock the door that will finance the preaching of the gospel in the last day, and you could be on the receiving end.

> For God giveth to a man that is good in his sight wisdom, and knowledge, and joy: but to the sinner he giveth travail, to gather

and to heap up, that he may give to him that is good before God. (Eccl. 2:26)

Did you know that the evil are working for you and they don't even realize it? Imagine working a lifetime to build up a nest egg, only to give it to someone else. But that is happening right now. To those who please God, God gives wisdom, knowledge, and joy. But Solomon says the sinner gathers and heaps up in order to give all he has to those who please God. (Notice that the translators render the word *heap* in both James 1:3 and Ecclesiastes 2:26.) If you please God—and you do if you belong to Him—then wisdom, knowledge, and joy are yours, as well as the wealth stored up by your unsaved neighbors and coworkers.

Of course, that doesn't mean you can march right into their homes and take what you want. But pray that God will bless them because eventually what they have gathered will fund, in part, the final harvest.

> And it shall be, when the LORD thy God shall have brought thee into the land which he sware unto thy fathers, to Abraham, to Isaac, and to Jacob, to give thee great and goodly cities, which thou buildedst not, and houses full of all good *things*, which thou filledst not, and wells digged, which thou diggedst not, vineyards and olive trees, which thou plantedst not; when thou shalt have eaten and be full. (Deut. 6:10–11)

Imagine yourself in city hall, standing before the media with pictures flashing, television cameras humming, and the crowd clapping. The mayor presents you with a key to the city. But this isn't a symbolic key, it's a real key. "Here is *the* key to our city," he begins. "It's yours. You are now free to use our grocery stores, shop in our malls, even go through our homes. You can go wherever you want, whenever you want, and take whatever you want at no cost because this city now belongs to you."

Sound far-fetched? Not to the breaker. God has promised that those who possess the land will inherit cities they didn't form, houses they didn't build, wells they didn't dig, and vineyards and olive trees they didn't plant. All this to finance the end-time harvest.

You have the opportunity to begin a financial revolution in your life. Through your actions, your life will be changed. No more debt. No more lack. But in order to realize this divine windfall, you will have to rise up with the spirit of a breaker. You have to break through something you've never done before. In order for you to have a future that is different from your past, you will have to change something you do today.

A breaker with overpowering wealth is not one who keeps the wealth, but rather one who shares the wealth. As you grow in the grace of giving, the spirit of the breaker will rest upon your gifts and break through every line of Satan's defense.

WHY NOT YOU?

Jesus Christ, our Liberator and Leader, the Breaker who goes before us, is sifting through the ranks of the self-satisfied and self-indulgent. He is searching for a remnant of third-day Christians who are ready to pursue, overtake, and recover all. Men and women with the valor to pass over and vigor to pass through. He is looking for people with the spirit of the breaker who refuse to be contented with life as usual.

People of this pedigree seek not the keys of an earthly city but possess the keys of a heavenly kingdom. And, whatsoever they bind on earth is bound in heaven, and whatsoever they loose on earth is loosed in heaven.

Like Joshua, they pass through troubled waters, track down their enemy, and then stand valiantly in the victory forged in the crucible of conflict that was originally designed to cause their ultimate demise.

Like Samson, who stripped the gates of Gaza from their hinges, these remnant believers cast aside every weight of sin that so easily besets them and every gate of hell erected to keep them from the promise of God.

Like Stephen, they love not their lives even unto the death. And for the bloodstained cross of Christ they offer themselves as living . . . and dying sacrifices.

These men and women do not shrink back because their confidence is hidden in the Breaker who goes before them, Jesus Christ. They know they are not the first to encounter trouble, because *He came first.*

So then the sons and daughters of Perez, strengthened by God's grace, break through every line of Satan's defense: sin, sickness, depravity, the devil, and disease. They force themselves through the narrow gate and endure hardness as good soldiers of Jesus Christ.

God will have a day, an hour, a moment when His people full of His Spirit are going to walk upon the face of this earth in absolute dominion. In these last days, the concern is not the what or the how, but the who and the when. Why not you? Why not here? Why not now?

Jesus isn't looking for those who claim perfection; He is looking for those with the desire to grow in virtue, valor, vigor, and overpowering wealth. But those who choose to take on this mission enjoy the plunder that belongs to the victor. They experience the pleasure that comes from participating in the coming kingdom. They encounter the pain that accompanies adversity but continue marching forward, knowing that when they fulfill their mission, they will win the prize.

Men and women of this ilk realize that the privilege of being a breaker is theirs only because the Breaker goes before them. Jesus Christ. *He came first.*

A revival *is* coming and you can play a part in it. God is about to put a new spirit in you—the Spirit of the Breaker. You will end up where you never dreamed you would be. You will give birth to a miracle you didn't even know you were pregnant with. The gates of brass and bars of iron will be broken in pieces before you, and the very gates of hell shall not prevail against you!

Why? Because you and I are the sons and daughters of Perez. We are the breakthrough generation! We are the Holy Ghost–filled, fire-baptized remnant church of Jesus Christ, and we are coming to a city near you!

NOTES

CHAPTER 1

1. Peggy Anderson, comp., *Great Quotes from Great Leaders* (Lombard, Ill.: Celebrating Excellence Publishing, 1990).
2. Bible Illustrator for Windows 3.0c, 1990–98, Parson's Technology, Inc.
3. R. Laird Harris, *Theological Wordbook of the Old Testament* (Chicago: Moody Press, 1999), s.v. "*halal.*"
4. Ibid., s.v. "*asa.*"

CHAPTER 3

1. Richard Whitaker, ed., *The Abridged Brown-Driver-Briggs Hebrew-English Lexicon of the Old Testament* (Oak Harbor, Wash.: Logos Research Systems, 1997), s.v. "*tselem.*"
2. W. E. Vine, Merrill F. Unger, and William White, *Vine's Complete Expository Dictionary of Old and New Testament Words,* electronic ed., Logos Library Systems (Nashville: Thomas Nelson, 1997).

CHAPTER 4

1. *The American Heritage Dictionary of the English Language,* 3rd. ed. (Boston/New York: Houghton Mifflin Co., 1992).

2. "Evangelicals Are the Most Generous Givers, but Fewer than 10% of Born-Again Christians Give 10% to Their Churches," April 5, 2000, Barna Group, www.barna.org.

CHAPTER 5

1. Harris, *Theological Wordbook of the Old Testament,* s.v. *"herem."*

CHAPTER 7

1. Harris, *Theological Wordbook of the Old Testament,* s.v. *"hayil."*
2. *Enhanced Strong's Lexicon* (Oak Harbor, Wash.: Logos Research Systems, Inc., 1995), s.v. *"zayo."*

CHAPTER 9

1. Harris, *Theological Wordbook of the Old Testament,* s.v. *"amar."*

CHAPTER 10

1. *American Heritage Dictionary.*

CHAPTER 11

1. Some of the historical background in the story was gleaned from Craig S. Keener, *IVP Bible Background Commentary: New Testament* (Downers Grove, Ill.: InterVarsity Press, 1997), Luke 4:16–30.
2. Henri Nouwen, *In the Name of Jesus* (New York: Crossroad Publishing Co., 1992), 62.

CHAPTER 12

1. Vine, Unger, and White, *Vine's Complete Expository Dictionary.*
2. The Hebrew word for "tongues" can also be translated "languages." For this reason some scholars wrongly teach that speaking in tongues is only a missionary gift, enabling people to travel to foreign countries and share the gospel in a native but unlearned tongue. This occurred at Pentecost when

people from foreign countries who happened to be in Jerusalem heard the gospel miraculously preached in their native language (see Acts 2:5–11). Throughout the history of the church and even today, reports indicate that God still uses people in this respect. But the gift of tongues is not limited to speaking in a known tongue. The apostle Paul refers to speaking in the tongues of men and angels in 1 Corinthians 13:1. If you speak in an unknown tongue or you would like to speak in tongues, don't concern yourself with the details of whether or not it is in a known language. The baptism of the Holy Ghost can be a missionary gift, but more importantly it *empowers* the missionary call in all of us to boldly proclaim the good news of Jesus, whether in a known tongue or unknown tongue.

CHAPTER 13

1.Robert J. Morgan, *Nelson's Complete Book of Stories, Illustrations & Quotes* (Nashville: Thomas Nelson, 2000). Additional information was obtained from The Handbook of Texas Online at http://www.tsha.utexas.edu/handbook/online/articles/print/T T/dot3.html.

CHAPTER 15

1. *Merriam Webster's Collegiate Dictionary,* 10th ed. (Springfield, Mass.: Merriam-Webster, 1994).

ABOUT THE AUTHOR

R OD PARSLEY is pastor of World Harvest Church in Columbus, Ohio, a dynamic church with more than 12,000 in attendance weekly that touches lives worldwide. He is also a highly sought-after crusade and conference speaker who delivers a life-changing message to raise the standard of physical purity, moral integrity, and spiritual intensity. Parsley hosts *Breakthrough,* a daily and weekly television broadcast seen by millions across America and around the world, and oversees Bridge of Hope Missions and Outreach, World Harvest Bible College, and World Harvest Academy. He and his wife, Joni, have two children, Ashton and Austin.

It's exciting to live right in the middle of God's divine preparation for a revolution. I have good news for you: You are on the brink, on the verge, on the precipice. You are about to be thrust into God's miracle for your life.

—ROD PARSLEY

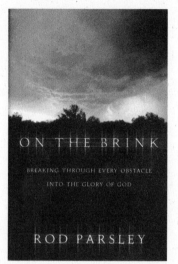

God is birthing a new kind of Christian—one who will be specially equipped for the last days, filled with His divine brand of power, conviction, grace, and mercy. Called "remnant believers," these spiritual giants will manifest and reveal the Lord's glory as never before as they bring the gospel to a suffering, sin-sick world.

Do you want to be a part of this holy revolution? If so, *On the Brink* is your call to arms. In this book, bestselling author Rod Parsley discusses days of unprecedented spiritual and social upheaval and what you must do to embrace your role as a remnant believer.

As we approach a time of spiritual revolution, preparing for the challenges ahead is essential—and possibly no other book will help you live victoriously as part of God's glorious church as effectively as *On the Brink.*

Ask for *On the Brink* at your local bookstore.

ISBN 0-7852-6808-1